Motiveless Malignity

by Louis Auchincloss

THE INDIFFERENT CHILDREN
THE INJUSTICE COLLECTORS
SYBIL
A LAW FOR THE LION
THE ROMANTIC EGOISTS
THE GREAT WORLD OF TIMOTHY COLT
VENUS IN SPARTA
PURSUIT OF THE PRODIGAL
THE HOUSE OF FIVE TALENTS
REFLECTIONS OF A JACOBITE
PORTRAIT IN BROWNSTONE
POWERS OF ATTORNEY
THE RECTOR OF JUSTIN
THE EMBEZZLER
TALES OF MANHATTAN
A WORLD OF PROFIT

Motiveless Malignity

LOUIS AUCHINCLOSS

LONDON
VICTOR GOLLANCZ LTD
1970

ISBN 0 575 00446 0

Printed in Great Britain by
Lowe & Brydone (Printers) Ltd., London

FOR ROBERT D. BREWSTER

AND THIRTY YEARS

OF FRIENDSHIP

Foreword

I DO NOT BEGIN with the conventional apology for adding my drop to the ocean of Shakespearean comment, because Shakespeare, the mighty idol of our culture, is entitled to the incense of every author coming after him. Writing about him has become like writing about life — and consequently about oneself. Shakespeare, at least, has nothing to lose.

Anyone who reads Arthur M. Eastman's splendid new history of Shakespearean criticism will become aware that he is also reading the history of English and American literature. The prevailing fashions are always reflected. Early in our century the cult of Shakespeare the playwright — the creator of characters and situations — reached its climax with Professor A. C. Bradley. The tragic heroes were analyzed as if they were actual persons with an existence anterior to their First Acts. It was perfectly proper to speculate on Lear's marriage, on Othello's bachelorhood, on Hamlet's college days. Iago's villainy was found to be motivated by his need to satisfy a greed for power in playing an exhilaratingly dangerous game. It is not surprising that such imaginative interpretation should have come at the end of the great era of fiction that began with Scott and Dickens. In our own day we have seen the characters, even Falstaff, subordinated to the cult of images. Shakespeare, the poet, has become everything, as might be expected in the age of Eliot and Pound.

There is no reason, however, why Shakespeare cannot belong to both, and to many more. It has been said that the only literary brew that would come anywhere near to producing him would be that of Dickens and Keats. My trouble with the extremists of character and images is that both require tighter habits of literary organization in Shakespeare than it seems likely that he possessed. To fit with their theories, he would have had to have blotted out far more than the thousand lines that Ben Jonson wished he had.

In recent years, I have tried to hew my way through the underbrush of comment and reach back to Shakespeare by reading him in facsimiles of folios and quartos. The variant spelling, the absence of stage notes, the running together of acts, the manifest errors in attribution of speeches help one to realize on what a huge body of speculation our modern concepts rest. It is like going back to the gospels after reading St. Thomas Aquinas. Half the plays were printed for the first time seven years after the poet's death and in some cases more than twenty after their initial production. When one considers further the Elizabethan habits of revising old plays and of collaborating with other playwrights, one has to concede that the finished product could not have been as meticulously constructed a piece as *Murder in the Cathedral.*

The first folio imposes nothing on us but the division of the plays into comedies, histories and tragedies, and even this we feel at liberty to reject. Why is *Cymbeline* a tragedy? Why is *The Winter's Tale* a comedy? I doubt if Shakespeare bothered himself with such classifications, and, if he did, I suggest that he used them only in the loosest sense, i.e., that tragedy ended sadly and comedy happily. Death, anyway, is all that the fates of Romeo and Richard III have in common.

The essays that follow are connected only in their tendency to speculate on the lack of apparent motivation in some of Shakespeare's principal characters. Sometimes, of course, this can be explained by stage tradition or necessity of plot. Sometimes, as already indicated, it may result from mistakes, either in Shakespeare or his editors. But it has been my growing conviction that in many cases, particularly in the later plays, it is a reflection of Shakespeare's sense of the perverse and irrational in human nature, a sense that I believe to have deepened with his experience.

Valentine in *Two Gentlemen of Verona* can offer his beloved to the man who has just tried to rape her because he is being true to an ancient conception of romantic friendship. The wicked Duke in *As You Like It* can suddenly repent and abdicate, and the Duke of Albany can forget about Lear and Cordelia after his victory, in order that their plays may end as planned. And King John's character is probably not clear to us because it was not clear to Shakespeare. But what about Capulet in *Romeo and Juliet?* Why does his desire to marry his daughter to Paris, tepid at first and subject to her consent, turn into violent resolution as soon as she refuses? Because he cares for his authority and not his daughter? There is more than a hint of sadism in such behavior. He is one of Shakespeare's early monsters, yet I suspect that to Elizabethans he may have seemed a perfectly normal, even a rather affectionate father. What is significant is that Shakespeare, unlike his contemporaries, saw him as we do.

The questions proliferate with the later plays as we move deeper and deeper into the human psyche. Why does King Lear react so unreasonably to Cordelia's small fault? Why does Macbeth have to kill Banquo? Why is Leontes jealous, without the least cause, real or apparent? Why does Hector join the war party against his conscience and judgment? Why is Timon such a willfully bad judge of character? Why does Coriolanus hate the poor so? Why does Iago destroy Othello? And why does he supply inadequate motives for his own malice?

It is from Samuel Taylor Coleridge's famous phrase in answer to the last question that I derive my title: "The motive hunting of motiveless malignity."

LOUIS AUCHINCLOSS

Contents

Motiveless Malignity

Othello – the Perfect Plot

THE SPEED with which Shakespeare was obliged to write his plays — at least thirty-seven in a period that probably did not exceed twenty years, or roughly two per annum — must have made his working day more like that of a television serial writer than of a serious modern dramatist. And what we know of his creativity does not cover possible lost plays and collaborations. Besides, he had his work as an actor, manager and producer. Not for him were the long modern periods of rustication. Not for him were the blessed opportunities of rejection and revision. Legend has it that he never blotted out a line.

Now it may be that this necessitated celerity was beneficial to his genius. He may have been one of those contrary souls who, with more time, would have struck out some of his best passages. What happened, for example, to the soliloquy "How all occasions do inform against me" between the quartos of *Hamlet* and the first folio? But there was one disadvantage from which he demonstrably suffered as a result of this tight schedule. If a chosen plot, a selected basic dramatic situation, proved unworkable, he was apt to be stuck with it. And such a plot, or situation, or whatever one chooses to call it — a character or characters presented with a problem — is more basic to the playwright's art than to that of any other literary man.

The novelist can cover a bad situation with a screen of words — modern French writers are even eliminating characters — and poets can be forgiven a bad stanza for a perfect line. But the playwright has no such leeway. He must be entertaining every single minute. His audience cannot skip; they cannot pick and choose; they cannot close him up and return to him in a better mood. They can only walk out. And to satisfy this heavy demand of attention not all subjects will do — they must be dramatic subjects. One could write a novel or a dramatic monologue about *Timon of Athens* — not a tragedy.

I realize, of course, that the theater in the 1950's and 1960's has been making all kinds of experiments with subjects that have not previously been considered dramatic, but these are essentially esoteric rather than popular, and Shakespeare was always a popular dramatist. He still is. You are more apt to see *Macbeth* on television than *Waiting for Godot*. Experiments in new dramatic techniques may be expected to change popular drama — they already have — but the ultimate response will always be a compromise, and that compromise is apt to contain more of the old than the new.

Shakespeare derived his plots from reading Holinshed, Plutarch and contemporary novels. The passage from the idea to its execution was probably rapid — sometimes on order, for a wedding or pageant, like *A Midsummer Night's Dream* or *Love's Labor's Lost*, or even on a royal request, such as Queen Elizabeth's legendary desire to see Falstaff in love — with two weeks to prepare it! As any author knows, sometimes the *donnée* (as Henry James always called it in his notebooks) is so perfectly adapted to the author's resources that it almost writes itself — those are the joyous, the perfect moments in his professional life. This happened, I think, with *Macbeth* and *Othello*. Then there are the *données* that are so hopeless that even Shakespeare could do nothing with them. This happened with *Pericles, Henry VIII* and *Timon of Athens*.

To dispose of the second category first, *Pericles* would probably never have been attempted had Shakespeare not been trying his hand at a new fashion. It is so rambling as to have no dramatic center at all, and it probably owed its surprising contemporary popularity to the extremely funny brothel scenes, which the nineteenth century rejected as Shakespeare's and which we feel to be indubitably his. *Henry VIII* we may try to blame on John Fletcher, but Shakespeare certainly had a hand in it. It represents an unfortunate return to the chronicle play:

the ending has nothing to do with the beginning, and the central characters, the King and the Cardinal, are drawn without even an attempt at consistency. The play, except for a few fine scenes for Queen Katherine, is a bore.

Timon, the last of the bad *données*, may be the one play that Shakespeare *did* abandon unfinished, tight schedule or no tight schedule. He must have seen that it was hopeless, and there is no record that it was acted in his lifetime. G. B. Shaw has criticized Shakespeare for spending so much energy on plot, and he has bemoaned the necessity of plot in the same way E. M. Forster has bemoaned it in the novel. But I look in vain among Shaw's criticisms for any laurels handed out to *Timon*, the one play of Shakespeare's that lacks a plot. Oh, yes, strictly speaking, it has one. Timon lavishes his money on his friends, loses it all, finds that his friends are false and becomes a misanthropist. But compared to the elaborate mechanics that govern the action of the other plays it amounts to no plot at all, and I do not see how there can be any question that this plotlessness makes the play tedious. One never feels the smallest sympathy for Timon himself, who is first a fool and then a bad sport. True, there is magnificent poetry in his denunciations, but a play needs more than this. The very existence of this poetry in the play is the ultimate rebuttal of Shaw's theory that the greatness of Shakespeare lies entirely in his music and that the plots and characters make up rather banal librettos. Poetry cannot save *Timon*, and this despite the fact that *Timon* in 1968 is probably the closest in spirit to our times of all the plays except *Troilus and Cressida*. Timon is an angry man of the modern English school, who exists to abuse.

But Shakespeare must have known at once, when the situations of *Macbeth* and *Othello* occurred to him, that he had subjects perfectly suited to his genius. Considered as poems I would rate *Hamlet* and *King Lear* higher than either, but considered as plays *Macbeth* and *Othello* are without peer in the whole canon. From beginning to end they are totally exciting.

A. C. Bradley has pointed out that *Othello* is the most "enclosed" of the great tragedies. There is none of the relief in it that we find in *King Lear* or *Hamlet* where the sufferings depicted are shown in some relation to more general suffering, where the agony of the central characters has some kind of place, even purpose, in a world that recognizes the role of man. The storm on the heath seems a response by nature to the crisis of Lear. But in *Othello* there is nothing to relieve the mind from the horror of the central spectacle of a man of high integrity and noble character moved to murder a wife whose virtue matches his own. The storm which scatters the Turkish fleet has nothing to do with the protagonist's passion. It is the prelude to the calm in which we can look for no distraction.

The range in opinion about the character of Othello goes from Bradley's conception of the totally magnanimous, diabolically deceived hero, to F. R. Leavis' interpretation of him as the victim of his own self-dramatization and self-idealization. I agree with both and see no inconsistency. Those who like to emphasize Othello's "fault" are those who dislike to view the tragedy as one of situation. They find more significance in a play where the hero is destroyed by himself than where he is simply the victim of a plot. Certainly Othello brought on his own destruction, but I do not think he could help it.

Shakespeare, I believe, thought that Othello the Moor should be judged, if judged at all, by standards very different from those applicable to the Venetian characters in the play. For he is totally alien to them. He is nobler, grander, braver, greater in spirit, but he is also more naive, more superstitious, more credulous, more subject to his passions. That such a man will kill when his jealousy is aroused was, I think, totally accepted by a Jacobean audience. I doubt that Shakespeare regarded Othello's jealous passion as a "flaw," but rather as a basic characteristic of Moors, who were considered to be very violent people, quite different from Englishmen or even Italians.

In this respect, it is necessary to make clear that the play is not involved with racism as we conceive of it in America in 1968. Many of the characters make it brutally clear that they find Othello's blackness physically repulsive, but none of them consider him a social inferior. They regard him as Victorian Englishmen might have regarded some splendid Maharajah. Othello is of royal birth; he is the military savior of the Venetian state; he dines on equal terms with the greatest senators and is well known to the Doge. But he is always a complete foreigner. The Venetian aristocrats will never admit him to their innermost society, and they certainly do not want their daughters to marry Moors. But then they probably would not marry their daughters outside of fifty families along the Grand Canal.

If Othello were a Venetian, he would indeed be an unpardonable sot for being taken in by another Venetian, even by one of such seeming honesty as Iago. For mark how little Iago need do before reducing Othello to desperation. In two dialogues, interrupted only by the brief appearance of Desdemona (who in that appearance does nothing to confirm Iago's accusations), Iago brings his master from a state of mind of total trust of his wife to one where he openly resolves to have Cassio murdered. To accomplish this, Iago offers no evidence but his own account of what he claims to have heard Cassio say in his sleep. And in one later scene, to bring Othello to the further point of murdering Desdemona, he has only to add the trick of making the Moor believe that Cassio (whom he cannot overhear) is speaking lewdly of his wife. This scene ends, quite coincidentally, when Bianca enters with a handkerchief — an action which Iago has not even planned.

Of course, Iago is not counting on the persuasive power of his evidence. He is counting on the total ignorance of the Moor of the customs of Venetian society. He knows that the easiest thing to make a simple foreigner believe is that a lot more is going on behind the gilded front of the great world than meets the eye. When he tells Othello that Venetian wives let heaven see the pranks they dare not show their husbands, the poor Moor can only gape and say: "Dost thou say so?" And where Iago makes his shrewdest and boldest stroke is in impugning Desdemona's chastity because of the abnormality of her falling in love with a black man!

I used to feel that he was going too far and that a man of Othello's pride would have thrown him out of the room for such a suggestion. But the more I read the play, the more I am impressed with Othello's naiveté and his sense of inadequacy (humility or inferiority would be too strong) before the Venetian nobility. He knows his own value — no man better — but he knows, too, that he is moving amid people whose motivations and moralities are a closed book to him. The greatest breakthrough has been Desdemona's love. Of course, it has come as a shock, however blessed a one, that this rare creature should love a man so alien, so black, so much older than herself. The world has become paradise, so to speak, in a day, but chaos under such circumstances is always just around the corner. Is it not more in accordance with what Venice has always *looked* like to Othello that Desdemona's love should really be a passing and abnormal lust for something novel? A perverse appetite for a different-colored skin?

Othello has already had a moment of suspecting that things are too good to be true. Greeting Desdemona in Cyprus he says:

> If it were now to die,
> 'Twere now to be most happy; for, I fear,
> My soul hath her content so absolute,
> That not another comfort like to this
> Succeeds in unknown fate.

Desdemona immediately protests that their loves and comforts should increase with their days, but we suspect already that Othello is right. For if Othello knows little about Venice, it is already evident that poor Desdemona knows little about Moors. Indeed, so great is her trust, so utter her devotion, so passive her attitude to her husband, that some commentators have found fault with her. But the idea that Desdemona may show a tragic flaw in her faint misrepresentation (or "tergiversation" as Mrs. Anna Jameson calls it) of the loss of the handkerchief, seems to me too tiresome to be rebutted. It should be perfectly obvious that Desdemona is entirely without fault in her own ill fortune, just as I believe that her husband is meant to be the helpless victim of his own simplicity and native violence. The important thing about Othello and Desdemona is not what they lack, but what they briefly have: the beautiful relationship of the first two acts. It is a perfect thing, finer even than what Romeo and Juliet have, and its destruction is the most painful sight in all of Shakespeare.

The question, then, of the tragedy is who or what destroys it. Is it really Iago? He is one of Shakespeare's most brilliant creations, but is he quite human? Does he even have a motive? No critic that I have read believes that Iago is motivated by jealousy of Othello or of Cassio with respect to his wife, or even that he is seriously put out by Cassio's being promoted over him. This latter promotion is probably the thing that irritates him the most, but we never feel that it is the true cause for so monstrous a retribution. As Coleridge put it, this is "the motive hunting of motiveless malignity."

There are human beings, of course, who are evil for the simple pleasure of being evil, but I wonder if they look and talk as normally as Iago does. It has always seemed to me that he is an almost impossible character to act, however fascinating he is to read. His lines to me, even when he is posing, do not seem to match what the other characters say about him. They cannot get over how "honest" he is. This note is struck again and again, as if his honesty were a kind of odd hat that he was wearing that one could not help but comment upon. Yet his demeanor and conversation do not seem particularly to suggest this characteristic. When he jokes with Desdemona and Emilia while they are waiting for news of Othello's ship, he is crudely cynical; it is obvious that he enjoys shocking Desdemona. Later, when he is talking to Cassio about Desdemona's personal attractions, he is almost lewd. Now cynicism and lewdness may not be inconsistent with honesty, but it does not seem to me that they are the traits that one might expect of a man whose honesty is so outwardly evident.

Then, for all the talk of his being a rough soldier, Iago gives a distinct impression of being highly sophisticated, and, finally, his conduct at the end, when he refuses to speak, is not easy to interpret. It always interests me that my desire for vengeance completely disappears with the discovery of Iago's crime. I have no wish to see him tortured in the last act, even though there are many moments in the third and fourth when I should be glad to. But Iago seems to cease to exist when his crime has been completed, which again raises the question in my mind as to whether he is really human. I find him at his most fascinating in his soliloquies where he seems to speak with a gusto and relish that is almost more diabolical than human. Iago *is* evil; he is the evil in man and in Othello — not because Othello is peculiarly evil, but because Othello is a man.

Would the Moor not have been bound to get into trouble with Desdemona anyway? Would a man so easily goaded not have been sure sooner or later to misunderstand something about her? Was this not the reason that harems were guarded? To me the play reduces itself in the end to a picture of a man destroying his own happiness — perversely, madly, as men do. I think that the terrible power of the last act lies in the utter truth and hopelessness of the picture. That is what Othello was; that is what Othello did. That is what Othello will do again. There is none of the relief of the final acts of *King Lear* or *Macbeth* or *Hamlet*. The death of Lear comes as a release, the death of Macbeth as a retribution, the death of Hamlet as the ultimate accomplishment of a task, but Othello's death is only the sending of the body after the soul that died with Desdemona.

Doctor Johnson stated his relief at finishing the painful work of editing this final scene, and Horace H. Furness, of the Variorum, candidly admitted that he wished that the tragedy had never been written. There is no utterance in Shakespeare more heartrending than Othello's last hopeless cry over the corpse of his wife:

> O ill-starr'd wench!
> Pale as thy smock! When we shall meet at compt,
> This look of thine will hurl my soul from Heav'n
> And fiends will snatch at it. Cold, cold, my girl?
> Even like thy chastity. O cursed, cursed slave!
> Whip me ye devils
> From the possession of this heavenly sight
> Blow me about in winds, roast me in sulphur,
> Wash me in steep-down gulfs of liquid fire —
> Oh Desdemona, Desdemona, dead, O, o, o.

Who is the "cursed, cursed slave"? I have never thought it was Iago. He has already ceased to exist. Othello's hell is to contemplate the result of his own hideous perversity, and ours is to see ourselves in him.

Lear's Shadow

When I was in college we were coming to the end of the critical school that sought for a flaw, the "tragic flaw," in the character of the protagonist of a tragedy. We were instructed that in Greek tragedies no flaw was necessary and that it was permissible for the tragedian to represent his hero as a mere plaything of the gods, although at times he could bring on an extra tempest of divine wrath by the manifestation of a quality called "hubris" which was a kind of defiance of celestial power or possibly mere vanity. But in the Renaissance a tragic hero had to provide his own undoing. Accordingly, we discovered that Macbeth was destroyed by ambition, Othello by jealousy, Hamlet by the inability to make up his mind, King Lear by the arrogance of trying to retain authority that he has given away, Antony by sensuality, Coriolanus by pride and, most oddly of all, Romeo by precipitateness. It has taken me a lifetime to unlearn these things.

King Lear is one of the few characters in Shakespeare

whose age is given. We know that he is over eighty. Gloucester, as the King's old friend, is presumably not too much younger although his having sired Edmund, who is represented as a very young man, may make him somewhat younger, particularly under the circumstances of Edmund's siring. We are never told why Lear's daughters are so young in relation to their father's age. Cordelia, being still unmarried at the opening of the play and a princess who would surely have been married well before her twentieth year, must have been born when her father was past sixty. Goneril, the oldest daughter, has no children but may be expecting one, so she is probably under thirty. It may well be that Shakespeare was deliberately dramatizing the conflict between youth and age by placing most of the characters in one or the other of these two camps. Kent, who is forty-eight, is the only representative of middle age (though Cornwall calls him "old fellow") unless we include the Fool who most commentators seem to find either a boy or an old man. The King, at any rate, is old, very old, and much older for 1605, the probable date of the play's composition, than he would be today. And the most important thing about him in his first scene is that he acts like an old man.

The division of his kingdom between jealous factions is an act of obvious political folly, and the assignment of shares in accordance with the professed loves of his daughters a manifest absurdity. I am aware that it has been argued that the division must have been mapped out before the action of the play commences, and that the pretty speeches are simply part of the formalities of abdication, but even if this is intended (which I doubt) Cordelia still loses her share by refusing to play the silly game. It seems to me inescapable that the Lear who so penalizes her is in the first stages of senility. Some commentators have found Cordelia's reluctance to go along with his mood to be a stubbornness, which is in itself her "tragic flaw" and furthermore one that must justly bring about her death in the last act. I cannot see that Cordelia is reprehensibly stubborn, and I consider her definition of filial love to be an exact and appropriate one:

> I love your majesty
> According to my bond; no more nor less.

When so frustrated, Lear bursts into irrational temper and in a few minutes disinherits and banishes his daughter and his most faithful friend and follower, the Earl of Kent. Goneril and Regan are under no illusions about his conduct, and, left alone, they immediately discuss how unreasonable he has been to cast Cordelia off. Regan points out that he has never but "slenderly" known himself, and Goneril agrees that the "best and soundest of his time hath been but rash," but here I think their spite is carrying them too far. I sense in the atmosphere of the play that Lear in his better days has been a good man and probably a good king, perhaps even a great one. Certainly, he has inspired the deepest loyalty in Kent, in

Gloucester, in Edgar and in the Fool. Albany respects him, and Cordelia adores him. But more than this, there is a majesty in his presence ("Ay, every inch a king!") which seems inconsistent with the projection into his past of his first act biliousness. To me his whole demeanor implies a long and splendid reign. It is hardly conceivable that a man of such outward authority and dignity could have ever been an inferior monarch. Extravagant perhaps, despotic, a Henry VIII, but never a Richard II. What I think is meant to appall us is how completely his form has survived his substance.

Although none of the characters ever says that he was a good king, the sources imply it. In *Percy's Reliques* we read:

> King Leir once ruled in this land,
> With princely power and peace,
> And had all things with hearts content,
> That might his joys increase.

Spenser says in *The Faery Queen:*

> "Next him King Leyr in happy peace long raind."

And from Holinshed we learn:

> *This Leir was a prince of right noble demeanor, governing his land and subjects in great wealth.*

In Shakespeare's first tragedy, *Titus Andronicus*, there is a parallel to the first act situation in *King Lear*. Titus, the hero and savior of Rome, chooses the worst of the two rivals for the imperial throne and slaughters his own son for opposing the marriage of the reluctant Lavinia to the bad candidate. Although there is nothing in the text to justify a reading of senility, a good deal is said about Titus' advanced age, and he is taken advantage of by the beneficiaries of his quixotically demonstrated loyalty in the same cruel fashion as is Lear. Could Titus at the height of his powers have been taken in by such shallow villains as Saturninus and Tamora? If he could not have been, the tragedy of the play must spring in part from the mental decline of the protagonist and the destruction to which such decline exposes him.

It has often been noted that in none of the fifty or sixty versions of the Lear story does the old King go mad, and I think that this has a considerable bearing on the question of senility. Not only does Lear go completely mad, but he fears madness for some time before it comes. It seems to me that a man would not be apt to fear madness because of a child's ingratitude unless he were already concerned with symptoms of failing mental power. In this respect I find the story of Sir Brian Annesley, a gentleman pensioner of Queen Elizabeth, fascinatingly relevant. In October of 1603 he was declared "altogether unfit to govern himself or his estate." Two of his daughters attempted to have him certified as insane so that they could get hold of his property, but the youngest daughter, Cordell, wrote to Robert Cecil, claiming that her father's services to the late Queen "deserved a better agnomination than at his last gasp to be recorded and registered a Lunatic." When Annesley died, his will was contested by one of the two daughters who had tried to commit him, but it was upheld. In 1608 Cordell married Sir William Harvey, widower of the dowager Countess of Southampton and hence the former stepfather of Shakespeare's patron. It seems to me almost impossible that Shakespeare should not have been acquainted with this story.

Gloucester, in the parallel plot, also shows symptoms of senility. He casts off Edgar, his oldest son and heir, on evidence that even Othello would have seen through and threatens to have him burned alive (the fate of patricides) if he catches him. There is no excuse for such appalling conduct except in the decay of his faculties. I do not mean to argue that the play is a brief for mandatory retirement at sixty-five, but I do believe that it is a study of the tragedy of incompetent old age in the toils of a ruthless younger generation. To me the theme of "nothing," sounded again and again, signifies the nothingness that Lear is becoming, as he declines to the nothingness of death. Caroline Spurgeon has pointed out that Shakespeare almost invariably associates death with negation. And the nothingness that lies imminently ahead seems to beget nothingness in the present: nothing to be given to Cordelia, nothing to be received from Goneril or Regan, not even *one* knight, nothing of comfort on the heath, nothing of hospitality from the castle, nothing of cover for the nakedness of poor Tom.

In the first scene in Goneril's castle Lear shows himself to be a very difficult and demanding guest. I have seen this scene played to show Lear's knights as perfect gentlemen and Goneril as an unreasonable and cantankerous hostess. I have also seen it played with the knights giving a faint sense of riot to an otherwise well-ordered household. It seems to me that the latter interpretation is more in accordance with the text. Lear's first remark as he enters with his attendants, of whom there are obviously a great many, is that he will not wait a "jot" for his dinner and commands that it be made ready. A few minutes later he shouts "Dinner, ho! dinner!" Then follows the scene where he strikes Oswald, Goneril's steward, and Kent trips him up by the heels. I perhaps strain a bit to find further evidence of the misconduct of the ex-King's entourage in a remark made by one of the knights to Lear. The knight says that there has been a great abatement of kindness not only in the general dependents, but in "the duke himself also," as well as Goneril. I do not see why the emphatic pronoun "himself" should follow this reference to the Duke of Albany unless it is meant to point out that even so kindhearted and tolerant a gentleman as Goneril's husband found the required housing of his irascible father-in-law oppressive. It is obviously vixenish of Goneril and her sister to strip their father of the retinue that was one of his conditions for abdication, but it does not follow that their desire to receive him with less of his knights is entirely unreasonable, nor is it beyond the bounds of possibility that they might have looked after the old man decently had he come to them with a sufficiently disquantitied train and been more civil to their staffs.

If Lear had a tragic flaw, in tragedy he would have to repent. What was it, and how does he repent? The only fault that he ever admits and for which he is bitterly regretful is the disinheritance of Cordelia, but this has been such a patent and shocking injustice that only a total lunatic, faced with his wronged daughter's overwhelming magnanimity, could fail to be ashamed. If Lear is to be regarded in Act I as a completely competent individual, surely his flaw must consist of arrogance and vanity. To split up his kingdom and award the biggest slices to the prettiest speechmakers and then to banish the two persons who dare to protest such folly is certainly pride at the very rim of the precipice. Yet I search the text in vain for a line to show that the King ever concedes that he has acted with arrogance. That he has brought death and destruction upon his kingdom never concerns him, because he is never really aware of it. He is totally preoccupied with what has happened to himself and is concerned only with paying back those who are responsible.

Insofar as Goneril and Regan are concerned, he is perfectly consistent, both in sanity and in madness, in his statements that he is a poor old man, as full of grief as age, a kind father whose frank heart gave all, a man more sinned against than sinning. His older daughters are vultures, wolves, pelicans, unnatural hags, who merit the most frightful curses. His mind constantly runs along the theme of revenge. He yearns to have his power back, and in his fantasies he imagines a thousand assailants come "hizzing" in upon his daughters with "red burning spits." Just before he is taken into custody and recovers his sanity he shouts:

> And when I have stol'n upon these son-in-laws,
> Then, kill, kill, kill, kill, kill, kill!

Much has been made of the fact that Lear in the storm learns that he is an ordinary mortal, like the least of his subjects, that he has taken too little care of poverty, that injustice abounds, even in his courts of law, and that hypocrisy generally prevails in matters of sex. A. C. Bradley went so far as to suggest that the play might properly be called "The Redemption of King Lear." But I think that this is taking the social consciousness of our own century and projecting it back to the era of James I. There is very little in any of Shakespeare's plays to indicate a concern with social welfare, and the ravings of Lear about the cruelty and hypocrisy of those in power and the misery of the poor wretches condemned by them have sufficient parallels in Jacobean mad scenes to make one wonder if it was not an expression of general misanthropy expected of a lunatic character on the stage. I do not mean to denigrate the tremendous power of Lear's denunciations, but I associate them more with his suffering than with any idea of repentance.

It is noteworthy that Lear's comments on social injustice are only vaguely related to the filial ingratitude from which he suffers and not at all related to any of his own apparent faults in Act I. Certainly, the denunciations of lust and pretended chastity seem unconnected with anything else in the play. Goneril and Regan are both lustful, but, so far as we know, Lear is ignorant of this, and they are certainly guilty of no hypocrisy in their brazen pursuit of Edmund. Lear's anger springs more from an old man's heartbreak than from a reevaluation of social principles.

In this respect a comparison of *King Lear* with *Timon of Athens* may be illuminating. Timon commands no sympathy because his generosity has been so willful, so flagrantly undiscriminating, possibly so egocentric that the indifference of his fair-weather friends in adversity seems not only anticipatable but almost deserved. Certainly his railing against the universe is out of all proportion to the ingratitude of the gang of sycophants whom he has pampered. Shakespeare, faced with this foolish aspect of Timon's behavior, may have tried to save the play by developing the willfully perverse side of his character, the basic need in Timon to destroy his wealth in order to create the ingratitude which will feed his self-pity, but even from this perhaps too twentieth century way of looking at the protagonist, he is still, dramatically speaking, a bore, and no amount of poetry can save the play.

But what concerns us here is Timon as a contrast to Lear. Timon and Lear both behave with reckless trust and generosity to obviously undependable people; they reap the whirlwind which everyone but they see coming, and they then excoriate the universe for their disillusionment. But there is a distinction, the distinction between a tragedy and a psychological case history. Our hearts bleed for Lear, while we simply shake our heads over Timon. One is a hideously tortured, infinitely pathetic old man; the other is an ass. Why? Because Lear at eighty is not really responsible for the conduct that leads to his destruction, and Timon, in his prime, obviously is. If Lear's senility is left out of the picture, his otherwise titanic wrath takes on some of the shrillness of Timon's, but if his anger is directed against a world that has produced at once the helplessness of old age and the remorseless fiends who take such cruel advantage of it, it becomes awe-inspiring. Lear does not condemn all mankind for greed and lechery just because his knights have been taken away. He has his vision, and a true one, of a race of cannibals.

The peace that descends upon the old King with the recovery of his wits under the loving ministrations of Cordelia, the calm after the storm, is a very beautiful thing, but I still see no signs of repentance or redemption.

Lear is bitterly ashamed of his treatment of Cordelia, as indeed he should be. He was not so senile as to be exempted from blame for that. But the other things, the trusting of Goneril and Regan, the splitting of the kingdom, the playacting as king with his noisy knights, even the exile of Kent, he has forgotten about. Why not? He should not be held strictly accountable for the irrational tendency of the aged to cling to their prerogatives while they shed their duties. That is their nature.

Lear in the end has found calmness and serenity simply in being looked after again by one who loves him and whom he deeply loves. Through the centuries audiences have found the hanging of Cordelia too dreadful, and in many acting versions it was repressed. But there is a kind of horrible rightness to it. The old man is spared nothing, as old people are so often spared nothing. Their capacity for pain may actually increase with their vulnerability. Beautiful things are shown in *King Lear:* Cordelia's love, Edgar's devotion, Kent's loyalty, but they can never sufficiently enlighten a scene darkened by the bestiality of Goneril, Regan and Edmund. The tragedy of the play is found in the commonest fact of life: the helplessness of the old against predators.

Works of art rarely have any direct practical effect on the lives of those who should most gain by them. I doubt that many would-be murderers have been warned off by the example of Macbeth or that many too hastily jealous husbands have profited by the example of Othello. But

King Lear strikes so directly into family life that I suspect that many parents since 1605 have had the old man's dread example in mind while considering settlements on their offspring. As a lawyer I can think of more than a few.

Hamlet's Delay and Madness

In neither of the two possible sources of *Hamlet*, Belleforest's *Hystorie of Hamblet* or the German play *Fratricide Punished*, which may be a version of the earlier English *Hamlet* referred to by commentators in 1589 and 1594, is there any indication that the hero was truly mad or that he was guilty of procrastination. It is made very clear in both cases that the madness was feigned in order that Hamlet might gain time in the seemingly impossible task of killing his powerful, well-guarded uncle. In Belleforest the hero says:

> *Neverthelesse, I must stay the time, meanes and occasion, lest by making over great hast, I be now the cause of mine owne sodaine ruine and overthrow, and by that meanes and before I beginne to effect my hearts desire. Hee that hath to doe with a wicked, disloyall, cruell and discourteous man must use craft and politike inventions.*

Hamblet, therefore, must actually use his will power to delay his revenge and not ruin all by haste. The Hamlet of *Fratricide Punished* goes so far as to demonstrate impatience with the Ghost who comes to urge speed, not reckoning with all the difficulties that mortals have to face:

> *Ah, noble shade of my father, stay! Alas! Alas!*
> *What wouldst thou? Dost thou demand vengeance?*
> *I will fulfil it at the right time.*

And at the opening of Act V he soliloquizes as follows:

> *Unfortunate Prince! how much longer must thou live without peace. How long does thou delay, O righteous Nemesis! before thou whettest thy righteous sword of vengeance for my uncle, the fratricide? Hither have I come once more, but cannot attain to my revenge, because the fratricide is surrounded all the time by so many people. But I swear that, before the sun has finished his journey from east to west, I will revenge myself upon him.*

I believe it is the consensus of the more esteemed critics that Hamlet is never really mad, but the books are filled with theories as to why he feigns madness. In the sources, of course, he uses insanity as a mask to his revengeful intent while he develops his plans against an enemy too powerful to be directly confronted. But Shakespeare's Hamlet seems at his most openly vengeful in the mad scenes. He tells Ophelia, when he probably knows that Claudius is listening, that those that are married, "all but one," shall live, and he protests to

Rosencrantz and Guildenstern that he lacks advancement. His madness seems designed rather to arouse the King's suspicions than to allay them. Dr. Johnson has correctly pointed out that Hamlet accomplishes nothing under the guise of madness that he could not have achieved without it.

Many have surmised that Hamlet uses the disguise of madness as a cover for his hysteria. But why should he pretend to be wholly mad because he is partially so? Dover Wilson has a most ingenious theory that Hamlet feigns madness to protect his mother from the scandal of the discovery of her first husband's murder and of her own adultery (he interprets the Ghost's use of the word 'adulterate' as meaning that Gertrude has been Claudius' mistress before King Hamlet's death). As the Ghost has enjoined him never to hurt Gertrude, he must bring down Claudius in such a way as to make the public believe that he has acted purely from ambition. Hamlet, seemingly crazed by Claudius' usurpation of the throne, will assassinate his uncle, Gertrude's reputation will be saved, and the Ghost will have been obeyed.

The trouble with this theory, as with all others, is that if Shakespeare had intended it, he would have made it clearer. He lived long before the twentieth century literary habits of obscurity. Ordinarily he went out of his way to drive his points home, and the plays are full of asides and soliloquies that are really not needed to clarify the text. Is any reader in doubt about Brutus' motives in killing Caesar or the reasons for the hypocrisy of Richard III? No character has more soliloquies than Hamlet or more opportunities to instruct the audience. If he never tells us why he feigns madness, it must be because it is not important for us to know. It is enough that we have the diversion of his assumed irrationality, and very diverting it is. Sir John Gielgud is the only Hamlet I have ever seen who took full advantage of the rich comic opportunities of the mad scenes. I can still see, after three decades, the telling glance that he shot at Polonius' nether regions as he uttered the phrase: "together with most weak hams."

Am I saying that Shakespeare had Hamlet feign madness to be funny? No — though he certainly never neglected any opportunity for a laugh. He was a man of the theater, first and foremost. I believe that he put in the feigned madness because it was in the sources (he was inclined to be faithful to such) and because his public liked mad scenes. It is interesting to note in this respect that he added madness to his picture of King Lear who in all the old poems and chronicles is perfectly sane. Also I note that Edgar in that play feigns madness, admittedly for the valid purpose of concealment, but far more than necessary. In fact, he continually risks drawing attention to himself to make a good mad scene. As I see Shakespeare's method, it was this: Hamlet pretended to be mad in the earlier play and in Belleforest; Hamlet pretending to be mad was good theater: ergo, Hamlet should pretend to be mad. That pretended insanity does not have the function in Shakespeare's tragedy that it had in the sources was something that he simply overlooked or ignored. But as pretended madness fits so perfectly with Hamlet's histrionic fervor and with his occasional near hysteria, it is never a fault in the theater and becomes a puzzle only in the library.

The second great issue in the criticisms of *Hamlet* is his supposed delay in killing his uncle. There is no similar delay in the sources; there the hero accomplishes his task as soon as he can, and against great odds. But Shakespeare's Hamlet seems to take a long time about it, and several distinguished but in my opinion rather bloodthirsty critics find this to be a fault or "tragic flaw." I doubt that the delay was intended by Shakespeare to be considered so close to the heart of his play.

Let us consider the bare bones of the plot. Hamlet is instructed by a ghost that his father has been murdered by his uncle. This shocking fact is known only to him and the guilty party, though it is later imparted to Horatio. Hamlet, surmising that his ghostly visitant may be an agent of the devil, is in a quandary as to how to proceed. Two months pass before the players give him an opportunity to test the King's conscience. The test proves the Ghost to be true, and Hamlet proceeds at once to execute his revenge. He discovers the King at prayers, defenseless, but passes up this chance because he wishes to damn him as well as kill him. The next chance seems to come immediately afterward when he hears an eavesdropper in his mother's chamber and kills Polonius, believing him to be the King. This is the fatal mistake that now throws the advantage to Claudius who is given his excuse to ship Hamlet to England with secret orders for his execution. Hamlet, with considerable courage and skill and an actual flair for action, outmaneuvers his uncle and returns to Denmark where he dispatches the villain at his first and only real opportunity.

It will be objected that Hamlet's doubts about the authenticity of the Ghost and his macabre scruples about the unfairness of killing his uncle at prayer are obvious excuses for putting off an act for which he has no relish, but he offers both explanations in soliloquies, and I take it as a rule that the soliloquy was designed to instruct and not to hoodwink an Elizabethan audience. A Shakespearean character may use the soliloquy for purposes of moralizing, philosophizing, speculating or informing, but never for misinforming. Hamlet can ask himself if he is a coward without being one; he can call himself a rogue, a peasant slave, an ass, a dull and muddy-mettled rascal without being any of these things, but when he states flatly that he must have better grounds than ghostly information before killing his uncle, I believe him. I also believe him, as did the horrified Dr. Johnson, when he tells us that an integral part of his revenge is the damnation of Claudius. Indeed this is almost an obsession of Hamlet's. He speaks of the pain of meeting his "dearest foe" in heaven, and he proscribes in his forged warrant for Rosencrantz and Guildenstern that they be put to death, "not shriving time allowed."

Unlike the reason for the feigned madness, of which there is no explanation in the text, there are three important references to Hamlet's supposed tardiness. The first is in the soliloquy: "O what a rogue and peasant slave am I!" in which Hamlet thoroughly berates himself for having waited so long (two months, it would appear, from Ophelia's calculation) before fatting the region kites with "this slave's offal." The second occurs when the Ghost interrupts Hamlet's colloquy with his mother, and Hamlet exclaims:

> Do you not come your tardy son to chide,
> That, laps'd in time and passion, lets go by
> Th' important acting of your dread command?

to which the Ghost replies:

> Do not forget. This visitation
> Is but to whet thy almost blunted purpose.

And the third is in the soliloquy: "How all occasions do inform against me and spur my dull revenge!" after the passage of Fortinbras' army, when Hamlet compares himself unfavorably with the adventurous Norwegian prince who leads his army to their possible deaths "even for an eggshell."

One could attempt to argue away the second and third

references by saying, in the case of the second, that the Ghost is not referring to Hamlet's delay but to his botching of the job of revenge by killing Polonius, and by pointing out, in the case of the third, that the "How all occasions" soliloquy does not appear in the folios. One might even argue that it must have been so omitted (despite the fact that it is the most beautiful piece of poetry in the play) because it makes no sense. How can Hamlet, unless he be really insane (and this is his sanest speech), declare that he has "cause and will and strength and means" to assassinate his monarch when he is under armed guard on his way to exile and (as he suspects) to his own execution? How can he anticipate the extraordinary luck of his escape in a pirate battle?

But I do not care for this kind of rebuttal. Shakespeare is full of minor inconsistencies. I think it is perfectly clear that Hamlet does accuse himself of delaying unduly. There is very little that Hamlet does not accuse himself of. He has something in him "dangerous"; he is "proud, revengeful, ambitious," with more offenses at his beck than he has thoughts to put them in. The two "delay" soliloquies are touched off, one by a spectacle of spontaneity and the other by a spectacle of action, both matters peculiarly upsetting to an intellectual like Hamlet. He is fascinated by the ease with which the First Player weeps over the fate of Hecuba and even more intrigued by the expedition of Fortinbras to conquer a piece of land that is not tomb enough and continent to hide the slain. Both men remind him of his own uncompleted task, and it is like him to berate himself. But this does not mean that we, the audience, are meant to consider a ranting player or a bloodthirsty and irresponsible aggressor as men better equipped to deal with life than Hamlet. The tragedy of the drama is not caused by Hamlet's delay; it is caused by Claudius' wickedness. Hamlet dislikes his task (as who but a callous Fortinbras would not?) and goes at it as best he can, full of doubts and self-reproach. But he gets there in the end.

And where has he got when he gets there? Claudius is dead, Hamlet himself is dead, and the kingdom of Denmark is turned over to the tender mercies of the brutal Fortinbras. Is it any wonder that Hamlet, brilliant and sensitive as he is, should have had doubts about the Ghost? I have had doubts about him myself. Did he come from hell to stir up a lot of trouble about a happily unknown murder? Well, of course, he didn't. Shakespeare was subtle, but he did not go in for that kind of Jamesian twist. Yet as Harry Levin has so brilliantly brought out in his *The Question of Hamlet*, the tragedy is a complex of questions. In the shifting sands of its marvelous dialogue one is never very sure of any ground.

Why, then, pursuing my own argument, did Shakespeare write so long a drama about a man's pursuit of revenge if delay was not an essential part of his plan? I suggest that the answer is that in putting Hamlet together he was more interested in the protagonist than in the plot. He was creating the man who has become the most interesting character in dramatic history, and he did not mean to sacrifice a jot of him to structure. What does it matter that Hamlet has no need to feign madness so long as it is in character for him to do so? And to reduce matters to their simplest terms, is it not better to have him delay his revenge than bring the play to an end?

I was struck in reading William Redfield's *Letters from an Actor* that Sir John Gielgud never gave Richard Burton (at least to the knowledge of one very close observer) a "theory" of *Hamlet*. And thinking back on Sir John's own peerless performance in the 1930's, it occurs to me that the very reason that it was peerless may have been that he did not have a theory. He simply played Hamlet as a character to the fullest in each scene without worrying unduly about pulling them together. And then, of course, they pull themselves together. Because that is what the play is about. Hamlet!

The range of the Prince is unparalleled even in Shakespeare's characters. He is one of the few with a pre-play existence. We know that he has been a brilliant student, an accomplished scholar, a man of exquisite courtesy and regal generosity, loyal, tender and passionate, who has been turned to a brooding melancholic by his father's death and his mother's remarriage, and then again turned to a savage, almost sadistic cynic by the discovery of his uncle's crime. Hamlet becomes more an avenging devil than an angel in his hatred and total disillusionment, and yet, before the end, he has managed to attain a serenity and charm that make Horatio's farewell heartbreakingly appropriate.

✧

And yet, having said all this, I still have a "theory" of *Hamlet,* but I offer it, not as Shakespeare's, but as my own. I doubt if my idea was ever in his mind, yet *Hamlet* is so rich a foundation that it seems to invite all the world to build upon it. So why should not I?

As I see Hamlet, he is a man removed from other men by a failing (judged by the world's standards) that is as rare as it is dangerous: the inability to forget. He cannot live altogether or even largely in the present; he cannot forget that his father was a great king, beloved of all, and that his mother has remarried within a month of his death. Hamlet's is the one suit of mourning in a gay court.

Nobody else gives a damn. King Hamlet may have been a very fine man, but he is dead, and King Claudius is a perfectly adequate successor, of royal bearing and demeanor, who handles the Fortinbras crisis with competence and dignity. Besides, the Queen obviously adores him, and who should mourn further than the widow? Polonius is high in the graces of the new monarch; Laertes, who has come dutifully to his coronation, is cheerfully returning to his studies. All is well. I cannot agree with Dover Wilson who says that Claudius usurped the throne and that all Elizabethans would immediately understand this.

Mr. Wilson claims that the word "election," with respect to Claudius, means no more than the consent of the Council to the succession of the new monarch, which was a necessity under English law. But there must have been a distinction, even then, between the ratification of a royal council, presumably unanimous, and an "election." The latter word was not unknown to Elizabethans. The Holy Roman Emperor was elected. So was the Pope. In Shakespeare's fictional Denmark it seems to have been up to some kind of parliament to select a successor to the crown, probably from among the royal family, but not necessarily by strict rules of primogeniture. Apparently the same system existed in Norway, for even the warlike Fortinbras seems to have been passed over in favor of *his* uncle. Hamlet had a claim to the throne, but Claudius had beaten him out. Very likely the Queen's influence was decisive. Hamlet is shown as very conscious of what he has lost, but not as considering it a great wrong. That Claudius has "popped in" between the election and his hopes is the least of Claudius' sins to his eyes. And nobody else seems to consider Claudius a usurper. There is none of the sullen atmosphere in the court that hangs about that of Richard III or Macbeth.

As the play opens Hamlet has no real grudge on which to hang his melancholy. It is disgusting and beastlike of his mother to have remated with such dexterity and nauseating that a world that has known and appeared to appreciate such a man as his father should accept his successor with such equanimity, but there is no crime in it. It is the way of the world, and Hamlet knows it. He hates the world for being as it is, and he wants to be out of it, but he has to recognize that *he* is the one who is out of step. The Queen hits his sorest nerve when she uses the word "seems" in her question to him. His reply is passionate.

> "Seems, Madam! Nay, it is; I know not 'seems.'"

You all are the seemers, he means. He alone is true. And then he discovers on the ramparts from the Ghost that this "normal" world is in fact, as he has dimly suspected, based on crime. Claudius and Gertrude are adulterers, and Claudius has killed his father. When the Ghost disappears, Hamlet is half hysterical. He jokes and equivocates with Horatio and Marcellus; he uses "wild and whirling words." I make out an exhilaration in this scene, a savage exhilaration, and why not? It is heady business to find that the complacent, nodding, bowing, banal world, the pompous showy world of Claudius, the world of windy speechifying about reason's common theme being the "death of fathers," is wrong, and that he, Hamlet, the sole mourner, has all along been right. The theme, after all, is not death of fathers, but murder of fathers!

After the exhilaration come doubts. The world goes right on in the same way. Even Ophelia joins it, falling in with her father's plans and sending back his letters.

Ophelia, like everyone else, assumes that a young prince can be intent only on seduction. Was the Ghost the devil's agent? Even if his father *was* murdered, does anyone care now? Anyone but he? What is revenge to a world interested only in the status quo?

Hamlet again contemplates suicide. How as simple a soliloquy as "To be or not to be" can be interpreted by some critics as "To kill the King or not to kill him" is incomprehensible to me. Then come the players, and he sees at last how he can resolve his doubts about the Ghost. And when his plan works, when once again he sees the evidence that the world is, after all, as he and not as the others have conceived it, a world based on murder, fraud and incest, he is seized again with that wild exultation that he felt on the ramparts. He cries to Horatio:

> Would not this, sir, and a forest of feathers (if the rest of my fortunes turn Turk with me) with two Provincial roses on my razed shoes, get me a fellowship in a cry of players, sir?

Now he will kill, but not to send Claudius to heaven. No, damnation is for the damnable. Has he not heard from the proved-honest Ghost of the horrors of Purgatory for an unshrived soul? So he leaves Claudius to his prayers and goes on to his mother's chamber where he later kills Polonius, thinking him the King. The Ghost appears again and reproves him for his delay, but it must be remembered that the Ghost cannot be expected to be sympathetic with Hamlet's having taken two months to test his story. The Ghost expects to be believed.

After this, as has been pointed out, Hamlet moves toward his revenge as fast as he can. The odds are now against him, but he overcomes them. It has been argued that Hamlet's task could not have been a difficult one, as Laertes upsets the rule of Claudius so easily, but Laertes has the unpunished murder of Polonius as his rallying cry which Hamlet could hardly use. Hamlet's wrong is known only to Hamlet, Horatio and the King. It is only when he himself is fatally stricken that he has his chance, when Laertes' public declaration of the King's guilt for this second murder stuns the onlookers, to make his final lunge at the villain of the piece.

Yet from the moment of Hamlet's return to Denmark there is a noticeable change in his mood. He is calmer, more resigned, more accepting. Except for the brief leap into Ophelia's grave, he seems willing to let events take their course, as if he were now satisfied that this course could lead only to the general immolation of the final scene. He speaks only once of his revenge when, after divulging to Horatio the iniquity of the King's English scheme, he says:

> Does it not, think thee, stand me now upon?
> He that hath kill'd my king, and whor'd my mother,
> Popp'd in between th' election and my hopes,
> Thrown out his angle for my proper life,
> And with such cozenage — is't not perfect conscience
> To quit him with this arm? And is't not to be damn'd
> To let this canker of our nature come
> In further evil?

Horatio warns him that he will have little time to do it, and Hamlet simply replies: "It will be short. The interim is mine." What does this mean? To me it sounds as if Hamlet were trying to argue himself out of the apathy that has descended upon him since the febrile activity of the English journey, as if he were trying to convince himself that revenge was still a valid goal. It seems futile to him, but he manages to bring himself to it, and in the end when the firebrand Fortinbras walks through a floor of corpses to a throne that has come to his unworthy self by default, we see just how futile it is. The world *was* right, after all, from the beginning; the status quo was better.

Yet the status quo was hardly worth preserving. That is what *Hamlet* says to me. The world of ready acceptance of immediate values, the world that does not want to overturn too many stones, the world that is intent only on getting on with the business of being the world is a fat, pursy creation without its conscience, which is Hamlet. No matter what suffering Hamlet may bring to it, he can still quicken it with a flow of energy and imagination that redeems it from nothingness. And so it is in our world today, in any world. Hamlet may be bitterness; he may at times be hate; he may in the end be a force of destruction, but he is always better than what he destroys.

Nemesis in Richard III and Macbeth

RICHARD III makes his first appearance, very briefly, in *Henry VI, Part II* and his second, at greater length, in *Part III*. I doubt if Shakespeare conceived of him as we ultimately see him in *Richard III* before the great soliloquy in the middle of *Part III* in which he suddenly reveals his total heartlessness and his decision to compensate for his crippled condition by playing a game for the crown against desperate odds. This sudden revelation of Mephistophelian planning comes as a complete surprise. For the first time the Richard that every Shakespeare reader knows is speaking. The soliloquy would do for the opening of *Richard III*.

Up to this point he has been shown as a loyal son and a brave, if rather savage warrior in battle. He is very much the leader among the sons of York, although not the heir, and he takes a strong position about his father and the crown, supporting the argument that the Duke should seize it with a sentiment that sounds like a weaker version of Tamburlaine's:

> And, father, do but think
> How sweet a thing it is to wear a crown,
> Within whose circuit is Elysium
> And all that poets feign of bliss and joy.

Only a very young man could think this of the crown of England in the fifteenth century. It is not a note that Richard strikes again. After this, he keeps informing us that he is without pity, love or tears, yet his actions seem to contradict this. He appears sincerely to mourn for his father and his brother Rutland, and he is certainly sincere in his anxiety for revenge and in his hatred of Clifford. After the revealing soliloquy he begins to show some of the bold humor and vigor of language that we are to see in *Richard III*, but he shows none of the antics that he will use in that play. There is nothing yet comic about Richard. Some time between the writing of *Henry VI, Part III* and the beginning of *Richard III* his full character must have appeared to Shakespeare, for his opening soliloquy in the latter play shows the peculiar combination of marble-heartedness, gaiety and wit that has made him the model of so many villains through the ages since.

As G. B. Shaw has put it, Richard is Punch. His arrogant rudeness and mock humility with the Queen's kindred is superb comedy. The beauty of Shakespeare's conception is that Richard has such confidence in his own strength of mind and will and such assurance of the asininity of his victims that he does not have to play his different roles convincingly. No, that would not be sportsmanlike; it would be shooting cows. The real fun of the game is to show the victim that he is being hoodwinked. When Richard says "I thank my God for my humility" or "I am too childish-foolish for this world" he does not expect to be literally believed. What he fiendishly understands is that all the silly world requires is that a role be *acted*. It does not in the least matter that everyone knows it to be an act. The Queen's kin must make do with the appearance of reconciliation; the Lady Anne with the appearance of courtship; the Lord Protector's council with the appearance of humility and piety; the Mayor of London with the appearance of the refusal of the crown. Richard, the spider, enjoys weaving his net with visible strands of silk before the very eyes of his flies. It is not so much deceit of which he is the master as hypnosis. Lady Anne is drawn to him by his very outrageousness. Laurence Olivier caught this aspect of Richard's character wonderfully in his film.

The glee with which Richard pursues his goal is contagious. In the first three acts one is almost on his side, as one is almost on the side of the villain of the film *Kind Hearts and Coronets* when he hews his way to a dukedom over a pile of corpses. It is difficult to be much concerned over the fates of the fatuously confident Hastings or of "perjured" Clarence or of the Queen's pushing kinsfolk. At times, as in the scene with the Mayor of London, when Richard enters between two bishops, reading a prayer book, the play approaches farce. But

Shakespeare's plot, dictated by history and hence not alterable in essentials, required a change in mood. Richard was a usurper, and he had not only to be destroyed, but destroyed by Shakespeare's sovereign's grandfather. This was no laughing matter.

It is a pity, for the play (too long, in any event) should ideally end after the crown has been achieved, with a quick comeuppance for the villain. Instead, Richard has to be excoriated for the monster that he is and England's salvation shown in the advent of the Tudors. The fun is over. It was convenient, at least, for Shakespeare that history also supplied the perfect event to change the mood of the play and to destroy any lingering sympathy an audience might have had for the protagonist. The murder of the princes in the tower does this job even better than the slaughter of Macduff's family does it in *Macbeth*. It need not even be done on stage. Shakespeare, who was not too squeamish to show us the eyeless Gloucester or Lavinia with her bleeding stumps, shrank before the sight of the smothering of those lovely boys. There are no more laughs after this deed is done. When Richard asks Tyrrel if he has seen the boys dead and adds "And buried, gentle Tyrrel?" we only shudder.

But after that we yawn. Richard is as dull in his unrelieved evil as Richmond in his unrelieved virtue. The change of mood has been fatal to the play. The long scene between Richard and the Queen, a parallel of the first act scene with Lady Anne, is a tedious replay with a much too anticipatable conclusion, unless one plays it (a possible construction) with the Queen only pretending to give in, in order to gain time and save her daughter for Richmond.

Some critics have seen in Richard's soliloquy after the visitation of the ghosts of all his murdered victims a splendid affirmation of his essential aloneness:

> Richard loves Richard; that is, I am I

and again

> I shall despair. There is no creature loves me;
> And if I die no soul shall pity me.
> Nay wherefore should they, since that I myself
> Find in myself no pity to myself?

I find the defiant parts of the soliloquy most effective and entirely consistent with Richard's character, but I wonder, even under the circumstances of the gloomy visitations, even with the prospect of defeat and death on the morrow, if the man who makes mock of his own hunchback after winning a Lady Anne in Act I and invokes the sun to shine out till he has bought a glass in which to see his shadow would have even broken down to cry "Have mercy, Jesu" or have been afflicted by his "coward conscience."

⟡

Richard III and *Macbeth* have the same theme: men of total egoism and colossal will power murder their way to the crown and alienate the world. At last that world rises to overwhelm them. In each play the sky seems to darken to a suffocating blackness, and then, just as one begins to lose breath, a strong clear dawn breaks. Once the retaliatory forces of society have been aroused, there is no further anxiety. One has never the slightest doubt that Richmond or Malcolm will triumph. One can see the avenging angel on the battlefield, with flourished sword, hovering directly over their heads. The two plays also fit together as the only two in the canon where the protagonist is so utterly evil that not for a single moment in the fourth or fifth acts does one want to see him prevail. We may have sufficient identification with Macbeth to hope, with him, that he will not be caught immediately after the murder of Duncan, but by the time Malcolm's forces are encamped before Dunsinane we look forward to their now inevitable victory.

Yet in *Macbeth* the interest of the audience that is caught up by the witches in the first scene is held, without abatement, to the final curtain. In *Richard III* much of the interest is lost with the change of mood. In *Macbeth* the mood is never changed. The nemesis which comes late in the earlier play appears in the very beginning of the other. Macbeth is a doomed man before he even commits his crime. He knows it, and the witches know it. It is what gives to this tragedy its deep and appalling quality. Macbeth does not go to hell; he starts there.

It is commonly said that Macbeth's fault is ambition, and he says of himself that he has no spur but "vaulting ambition." He wants, without question, to be King of Scotland, and this is certainly one aspect of ambition, but he never shows any other aspects. We are never told *why* Macbeth wants the crown. He does not, like Tamburlaine, think it "passing brave" to be a king and ride in triumph through Persepolis, nor does he ever indicate that he contemplates the least satisfaction from increased revenue or even from increased power over his fellow men. He seems to want the crown because in the dark, bloody, competitive world in which he must live it is an accepted thing for a man to want.

When he hears that he has been named Thane of Cawdor, he does not enjoy so much as a moment of exhilaration. He recognizes at once that this elevation has only brought him a step nearer to the terrible choice that he must ultimately make. I use the word "must" advisedly, as Macbeth constantly seems to regard the encompassing of the throne as a kind of dusky duty. He must move on to become a monarch even though his "seated heart" knocks at his ribs against the use of nature. His last hope of escaping the terrible obligation is that, if chance will have him King, then chance may crown him. But almost immediately afterward, when Malcolm is named Prince of Cumberland, he recognizes that this confirmation of the heir apparent throws the odds against his own peaceable succession of his royal cousin. There is to be no release now from his grim task. There is to be no easy way out.

In his letter to Lady Macbeth he speaks of sending her the news of his promised greatness by the witches so that she may not lose "the dues of rejoicing." But I note that the rejoicing is all to be done by *her*, and there has never been any rational doubt that she is ambitious, and in the crudest sense of the word. She wants to be Queen so that she may have sway over all others. She recognizes the cloudiness in her husband's motivation when she concedes only grudgingly that he is "not without ambition." She fully understands his inclination for that "even handed justice" that would commit the ingredients of the poisoned chalice to his own lips.

Although she says that he considers the crown the "ornament of life," she knows enough of his nature not to use any arguments that deal with the delights of that ornament. She knows just how to go about the job with a man as contrary as her husband; she has only to taunt him with not being a man. A man would seize the crown! She compares the deed with dashing a baby's brains out, only because one has promised to do it. It is unmanly not to perform one's promises, good or bad. Macbeth understands her entirely when he cries: "Bring forth men children only!" It may be even more a man's job to do a deed knowing beforehand exactly what one will have to pay for it. "In these cases we still have judgment here." He is never under the smallest illusion that there will be any fruits of his crime, and as soon as it has been executed he grasps at his doom, shouting "Macbeth shall sleep no more!"

Our next view into his mind is his soliloquy about Banquo. He has it all now, as Banquo says: King, Cawdor, Glamis, and for it he has given his "eternal jewel" to the common enemy of man. All this has been anticipated. Macbeth has expected no pleasure, and he has found none. But what he has *not* anticipated — or at least what he has not stopped to take more fully into account until now — is that he has done it all for the benefit of Banquo's issue. He has sold his soul; he was ready for the consequences of *that* bargain. But to have done it all for the advantage of the undamned, for the actual blessed, to have "filed his mind" for Banquo's posterity, is the devilish twist of fate that is simply unbearable.

It might seem that I exaggerate here. Why are Banquo's issue the beneficiaries of Macbeth's crime? After all, Duncan is ultimately succeeded by his own oldest son, Malcolm, as he presumably would have been had Macbeth allowed him to live out his normal life span. The Banquo line succeeded through genealogy rather than violence. But that is not the way Macbeth sees it. He has interrupted the natural flow of events, and by making one prophecy come true, he has implemented another:

> then Prophet like
> They hail'd him Father to a line of Kings.
> Upon my head they placed a fruitless crown,
> And put a barren sceptre in my grip,
> Then to be wrenched with an unlineal hand,
> No son of mine succeeding. If 't be so,

For Banquo's issue have I filed my mind,
For them the gracious Duncan have I murdered,
Put rancors in the vessel of my peace
Only for them, and mine eternal jewel
Given to the common enemy of man
To make them Kings, the seed of Banquo Kings!
Rather than so, come, fate, into the list
And champion me to th' utterance.

In his desperation he seems to be trying to undo the very mechanism that he believes that he has set in motion. But, of course, he cannot, for he has not set it in motion.

Here we have to take into account the full power of the witches. It is not a sufficient explanation, by those who dislike the introduction of the supernatural into human tragedy, to say that they are simply manifestations of Macbeth's wickedness. They play with human beings on their own account, and they directly affect the action of the play. It is true that Macbeth might have killed Duncan without their prophecy, and also true that he might have killed Macduff's family anyway and been killed in turn by Macduff without unearthly prognostications. But I doubt if he would have killed Banquo on the sole excuse that Banquo rebuked his genius, and he certainly would not have made such a point of trying to kill Fleance. The witches have to have a wicked man to work on, but having one, they can trick him into greater wickedness.

And now Macbeth gives himself over entirely to his frenzy, fighting on one mental level for a security that he knows he can never achieve ("It will have blood; they say blood will have blood"), and on another to light all the remaining fires of his hell. It is better to move ahead without thinking about it:

> Strange things I have in head that will to hand,
> Which must be acted ere they may be scanned.

He makes one more visit to the weird sisters, and this time they really put him on the griddle. After lulling him into a sense of false security, they confirm to him that all his crimes will redound to the benefit of Banquo's descendants, and he sees the happy, blessed issue of his victim parading in quiet, smug security across the stage, holding up balls and scepters to indicate their increasing dominion right down to King James I himself! It is enough to make any man mad. Once again he rejects thought for action: "The very firstlings of my heart shall be the firstlings of my hand."

The beautiful scene between Malcolm and Macduff that follows the murder of the latter's wife and children gives us a respite from blood and groaning and introduces a sense of high calm after frenzy. Shakespeare was a master at this; he does much the same thing in *Hamlet* after the Prince returns from the English expedition. I have always thought that the stage should be brilliantly lit for the Malcolm scene and that the performers should move across the boards with grace and dignity. The relief that we feel is the relief of knowing that there is, after all, sanity in a world that can be inhabited by such perverse creatures as Macbeth. It is not that we are allowed to forget in this scene what Macbeth has done. Far from it. The worst of his crimes is related to the horrified ears of the person most affected, but it is as if we were studying a disease in a laboratory and deciding with determination and assurance that the cure is in sight.

When the scene shifts back to Dunsinane, Macbeth is close to madness; he likens himself to a chained bear. He no longer has either our sympathy or our hate. He is simply a terrible wild thing, and the sooner he is put out of his misery, the better. By introducing the note of nemesis in the first scene of the play, so that the story is always soaked in the atmosphere of retribution, first anticipated and later richly experienced, Shakespeare has given to the old legend a peculiar and abiding horror. Macbeth knows that he will commit one terrible crime and suffer terribly. What he does not know is that he will commit countless terrible crimes and suffer unendurably.

The Tragedy of Antony

NEVER IS SHAKESPEARE'S famed fairness to both sides of a question more manifest than in *Antony and Cleopatra.* The tragedy is all Antony's, but Cleopatra, whose relation to his lust is that of Lady Macbeth's to her husband's ambition, rises in the end to tragic dimensions herself. She is a kind of Shylock, so magnificent in her total rejection of Roman (and English) virtues that she has made generations of commentators see the play as the triumph of love or a world well lost. Some twentieth century critics have even gone so far as to see the lovers as transcending earthly barriers and carrying their passion to Olympus to make the gods envious. But to Shakespeare she was always a whore, as Shylock was always a usurer, however splendid he made them otherwise. Is there any doubt that Antony is speaking aught but the literal truth when he says:

> I found you as a morsel cold upon
> Dead Caesar's trencher; nay, you were a fragment
> of Cneius Pompey's; beside what hotter hours,

> Unregister'd in vulgar fame, you have
> Luxuriously pick'd out: for, I am sure,
> Though you can guess what temperance should be,
> You know not what it is.

To Cleopatra temperance is for frumps; temperance is for Octavias. Her magnificence as a woman gives Antony the excuse he desperately needs to dignify his lust. For Antony has become the slave of passion. If Lear suffers from incipient senility, Antony suffers from something akin to satyriasis. It may not be the noblest of tragic flaws, but it is indubitably a flaw. This is apparent to every other character in the play, and, indeed, to Antony himself. Philo makes it clear in the very opening lines of the play:

> Nay, but this dotage of our general's
> O'erflows the measure . . .
> . . . . his captain's heart,
> Which in the scuffles of great fights hath burst
> The buckles on his breast, reneges all temper,
> And is become the bellows and the fan
> To cool a gypsy's lust.

Antony, receiving the first bad news from Rome, echoes Philo in saying that he must break his Egyptian fetters or lose himself in "dotage." Not only does he fully recognize the nature of his attachment to Cleopatra; he is far from ready to sacrifice the world for love. One cannot keep Egyptian queens in cottages. Both he and Cleopatra are very keen on retaining every square inch of their earthly dominions. When he sues to Caesar for permission to let him breathe "a private man in Athens," it is only because he has been defeated, and even then Cleopatra seems to wish to retain her crown, craving it for her heirs.

It is just as well for Antony that Caesar refuses his suit. He is better off dead than a private man in Athens. For Antony must always be the first among men. As he senses his temporal power slipping away, he seeks desperately, like Richard II, like Lear, to dignify his own degradation. What he still has must be made to look greater than what he is doomed to lose. If he must fail as a warrior, he must triumph as a lover. His performance in bed must equal that in the battlefield. "Kingdoms are clay," he tries to persuade himself. "Let Rome in Tiber melt." It is not worth the act of copulation.

But it would not be worth giving up a kingdom for the copulation of ordinary mortals. Oh, no. It must be Antony embracing Cleopatra; *that* is different. At that game, at least, they are peerless:

> the nobleness of life
> Is to do thus; when such a mutual pair
> And such a twain can do't

This is the essence of Antony's tragedy, expressed in the first scene of the play: the pathetic effort of an old reveler to equate his present performance in bed with his former conquest of the world. Of course, he knows in his heart that it is a farce, for at the first serious bad news he resolves to break with Cleopatra. It is too late. Cleopatra is wise enough to let him go — she knows just how far she can hold him — but in a single scene she converts his going from an abandonment of his mistress to an embassy at her command. Antony leaves Egypt her soldier, determined to return. Once in Rome, of course, he tries to delude himself that he can throw her over, marry Octavia and return to his old life as the "triple pillar of the world." But by now that is hopeless. He is bound to return to Cleopatra and to his ruin.

The seesaw between victory and defeat that follows the Battle of Actium prolongs the action unduly. I think Shakespeare was being too faithful to Plutarch here. I fail to see what we gain in knowledge of Antony or of the Queen in the brief respite that one victory affords them. Everything occurs twice: Antony twice plans a final revel before a next day's battle; he is twice defeated at sea through the cowardice of Cleopatra's fleet, he twice reviles her for it, and the play ends in two suicides, hers following his. The cosmic sweep of the first three acts with their sense of the Roman Empire pitted against the lovers is tediously reduced to a series of confusing frays. It is a good illustration of Shakespeare's borrowed plot backing up on him. But all is redeemed by the splendor of the death scenes.

If the low point of Macbeth's evil is touched with the slaughter of Macduff's family, the low point of Antony's fortunes comes in his consultation with Cleopatra in his battle strategies. That the greatest warrior of the world should bring his mistress to the front and twice put his faith in her fleet shows how besotted he has become. Enobarbus is rightly disgusted:

> If we should serve with horse and mares together
> The horse were merely lost; the mares would bear
> A soldier and his horse.

We can always trust Enobarbus to describe in graphic terms precisely what is happening to his beloved but declining leader. Yet Antony will fool him in the end. Reason and common sense dictate the abandonment of a general who has sacrificed his cause and his followers to a "gypsy's lust," but what Enobarbus has not counted on is the resurrection of the old Antony in defeat. His magnanimity in sending Enobarbus' treasure after him will destroy the deserter.

Antony doomed is not only generous to Enobarbus; he shows the same open and noble heart to all his followers, when he urges them to leave him. And his attitude to Cleopatra changes, too. Except when he is angered by her allowing Thidias to kiss her hand, and, just before his suicide, when, half-crazed with the humiliation of her fleet's surrender, he suspects that she has sold him to Caesar, his feeling is tenderer and simpler than in the preceding acts. There is less cosmic imagery now in their embraces. He is a soldier, even if a defeated one; she is his woman.

> Dost thou hear, lady?
> If from the field I shall return once more
> To kiss these lips, I will appear in blood.

He allows her to help him don his armor, compliments her playfully and in parting says: "Fare thee well, Dame. Whate'er becomes of me, this is a soldier's kiss." Returning from the battlefield, where the tide has briefly turned in his favor, he boasts to her:

What, girl! though grey
Do something mingle with our younger brown, yet ha' we
A brain that nourishes our nerves, and can
Get goal for goal of youth.

Humility comes to him in defeat and death. It is enough that he and Cleopatra are simple humans, mortal lovers. The references to envious gods are less boastful, almost playful:

Where souls do couch on flowers, we'll hand in hand,
And with our sprightly port make the ghosts gaze.

And when he sees her once more, unexpectedly alive, his concern is all for her welfare and how she must deal with Caesar and whom she must trust. But he does not die like Romeo, with a kiss. His last thoughts, more like Othello's, are for his reputation. It is not in Egypt that he would be remembered, but in Rome, not as a lover, but as a warrior. It is not as the infatuated fool who threw away his kingdom for a woman that he would go down in history, but as the triple pillar of the world. His last words refer back to the days before he met Cleopatra:

The miserable change now at my end
Lament nor sorrow at; but please your thoughts

In feeding them with those my former fortunes,
Wherein I liv'd, the greatest prince o' th' world,
The noblest; and do now not basely die,
Not cowardly put off my helmet to
My countryman, — a Roman by a Roman
Valiantly vanquished.

Cleopatra's reaction to defeat and death is just the opposite to Antony's. Her language, her images become more and more imperial, for the hour that is Antony's lowest is her finest. As she has never been a warrior, there is no humiliation in a lost battle. All her life of wiles and pleasure is redeemed in the splendor of her leave-taking. When Antony is borne in she cries:

O sun!
Burn the great sphere thou movest in; darkling stand
The varying shore o' th' world,

and again

Had I great Juno's power,
The strong wing'd Mercury should fetch thee up
And set thee by Jove's side.

When he dies, she exclaims, "The crown o' th' earth doth melt." It is true that immediately afterward she likens herself to a woman commanded by such poor passion "as the maid that milks and does the meanest chares," but I suspect this is one of her charming and royal affectations, and that if Iras or Charmian should venture such a comparison they would fetch up with a box on the ears.

Antony is dead; his disgrace is over. Caesar has won, as was always not only inevitable but politically desirable, and the Augustan Age is ushered in, the realm of universal peace. Now we can contemplate with detachment, and, as Octavius himself allows, with pity, the end of that fascinating, golden serpent who has brought the wonder of the world to nothing. For a brief moment Cleopatra exerts her wiles on Caesar, but it is only a dying flicker. She has essentially resolved to die as she has lived—royally. And in doing so she has the only revenge on Rome that is possible for her, for she places the finishing touches on her portrait of a civilization (if that is the word) so different from that of Rome that by Roman standards it can have no valid existence at all, a civilization where tragedy as Romans (and perhaps Jacobeans) conceive it does not exist, where lovers can prevail in the transcendent glory of their passion over dry and loveless Octaviuses. And on this note the play ends: so long as there is an Egypt and so long as there is a Rome, and so long as their circles intersect, what has just happened must happen. But I have little doubt that if Shakespeare had to choose, he would have chosen Rome.

War Aims in Troilus and Cressida

TROILUS AND CRESSIDA has enjoyed a steadily increasing popularity since the First World War. A world where women are faithless and men are fools enough to fight for them made total sense to the generations that grew up amid the disillusionments of the twentieth century. The railings of Thersites (whom I have always found a bit of a bore) have raised Shakespeare in the eyes of some moderns to the level of Beckett and Ionesco.

It has been popular to conceive the lineup of the two opposing armies, Greeks and Trojans, as that of heartless modern might pitted against ancient chivalry, of the cynical opportunism of power politics against an outmoded code of honor, of Machiavelli against Lancelot. The Greeks are wily, cynical, aggressive invaders; the Trojans, heroes of a hopelessly lost cause. Indeed, under this interpretation the Trojans are reminiscent of the Confederates, gallant but doomed, and Hector's election to go on with a war which he knows can have but one issue suggests Robert E. Lee's last-minute decision to stay with his native state.

Certainly Shakespeare has made his Trojans more attractive than his Greeks. Hector is heroic, and Aeneas noble. Troilus has charm and faith and courage; Priam has dignity. On the other side, Agamemnon is pompous, Ajax an ass, Diomedes contemptible and Achilles vile. Menelaus and Nestor are the targets of jokes, and even Ulysses, the best of the lot, is slightly dehumanized by his role as chorus.

But for all of this I still cannot find anything in the play to indicate that the Greeks have any motive for the destruction of Troy other than the recovery of Helen, which in mythology was presumably a justifiable one. Hector himself makes this concession in Priam's council when he demonstrates that the Trojans have broken a fundamental moral law. But having stated the case with clarity and eloquence, he then chooses to range himself on the side of the lawbreakers for motives of confessed sentimentality:

> What nearer debt in all humanity
> Than wife is to the husband? If this law
> Of nature be corrupted through affection,
> And that great minds, of partial indulgence
> To their benumbed wills, resist the same,
> There is a law in each well-ordered nation
> To curb those raging appetites that are
> Most disobedient and refractory.
> If Helen, then, be wife to Sparta's king,
> As it is known she is, these moral laws

> Of nature and of nations speak aloud
> To have her back returned. Thus to persist
> In doing wrong extenuates not wrong
> But makes it much more heavy. Hector's opinion
> Is this in way of truth. Yet, ne'ertheless,
> My spritely brethren, I propend to you
> In resolution to keep Helen still;
> For 'tis a cause that hath no mean dependence
> Upon our joint and several dignities.

Here Hector, in the last four lines, chooses to abandon order, principle and precedent for the "dignities" of Troy. He takes the side that he feels not only wrong but doomed, condemning his family and native town to destruction in order to save face. The Trojans, then, are united and chivalrous in a bad cause; the Greeks envious, factious and mean in a good one. And the good cause is bound to prevail, no matter how undeserving its supporters. From this point of view the play takes on a decidedly uncynical appearance. It might almost be called pollyanna. The good cause must always win.

Except that Shakespeare never leaves us there. As in *Hamlet,* nothing is left unquestioned. The cause that may have been good in mythology may not be good now. Can it be a good cause to return a whore to a cuckold? Shakespeare's love of balancing the equities has led many of his readers through the ages into error. Shylock is perhaps the most famous example of this. I do not believe that Shakespeare ever intended that the money-lender's splendid speeches on racism should blind us to the fact that he is as cruel and calculating a villain as Iago. Similarly, I do not believe that the worthlessness of Helen and Menelaus is meant to vitiate the fact that Paris has broken a fundamental law of society and that the Trojans have chosen to share his guilt by endorsing it.

Ulysses sees this and sees that society in the long run is bound to reverse the anarchic trend of Paris' rape. This recognition is attended by no contempt for the Trojans; on the contrary, Ulysses respects Hector and goes out of his way to perform the thankless but needful task of opening Troilus' eyes to his lover's infidelity. He is aware of all the divisions in the Greek camp, and he shows great ingenuity and statesmanship in patching the holes. But he is a long way from any sense of jingoism. He is a wise man, and well meaning, if detached. Destiny is on the side of the Greeks, and it is the role of the statesman to smooth the path of destiny, but it is not necessarily a function that a civilized man wants to crow about. When he talks to Hector about the inevitable end of the war, there is no gloating in his tone. Hector has chosen to remind *him* of their first meeting, and it is natural, under the grim circumstances, that Ulysses should repeat his grim prediction:

> Sir, I foretold you then what would ensue.
> My prophecy is but half his journey yet;
> For yonder walls, that pertly front your town,
> Yon towers, whose wanton tops do buss the clouds,
> Must kiss their own feet.

As usual in Shakespeare, the plot of the lovers echoes the greater plot. Troilus is a noble prince, but he is in love with a whore. As in Priam's council he is the loudest of all for the continuance of hostilities, making an actual virtue out of the slightness of the Trojan cause, glorying in fighting for the beauty and freshness in Helen that "makes stale the morning," so does he bring the passion and faith of a Romeo to the service of a wanton. Troilus is the very spirit of Troy; he is the symbol of the rotten cause in the gallant battle. Hector sees his lunacy clearly:

> 'Tis mad idolatry to make the service greater than the god.

Yet he goes along with his hotheaded junior. They all do. No one in Priam's council, for all their gallantry on the battlefield, has the guts to stand up against the ranting of a mad young prince who taunts his brother Helenus with cowardice for venturing to argue that Helen is not worth a war. And they all know just what Helen is, too! We see her, good-natured and giggling, obsessed with her jokes and her good times, a light-headed, loose woman totally indifferent to the slaughter she has caused. Why not? Had *she* ever asked anyone to fight over her? She would have gone to the Greek camp as complacently as Cressida and bussed every one of their leaders quite as prettily. She and Menelaus are probably destined to have a happy old age together.

Here Shakespeare seems to be saying something deeper about chivalry. He is not simply stating that the chivalrous men have the bad, hence the losing cause; he is suggesting, I think, that there is some inevitable connection between their chivalry and the poorness of their cause. Underneath all the talk of honor and the zest in fighting for it, is there much more than a dangerous pugnacity? And isn't this pugnacity the very despair of civilization? Hector suggests that Troilus is a hothead of the type Aristotle found unworthy of philosophy. Troilus is actually satisfied with Helen as a cause for bloodshed; he asks no better:

> She is a theme of honour and renown,
> A spur to valiant and magnanimous deeds.

Yet he too knows what Helen is, or should, unless he has blinded himself. We know that she has plucked a hair from his chin and that they have talked wantonly together. Yet he will *kill* for this woman! Small wonder that he picks a like one for himself. And when he finds her faithless, what can he do but go on killing?

Oh, yes, these are the gallant lords of honor, and what do they bring about but death and lechery? Troilus, like Hotspur, prefers war to peace. It is hard enough on those who have a stake in the struggle; but what about the poor foot soldiers whom Pandarus calls "crows and daws"? Not for them are the services of his compliant niece. They will share the miseries of defeat but not the spoils of victory. Their only hope, if they have any at all, is not in the glorious extravagant warriors, the Hotspurs, the Troiluses, who would blow up the world for glory — or hate — but in the statesmen, the Cecils, the great pragmatists of the Jacobean age. When I consider Ulysses, who has censors to read Achilles' correspondence and who knows how to make men act, I am reminded, not of Machiavelli, who is rather wearisomely cited in every discussion of sixteenth or seventeenth century statecraft, but of Richelieu — a young ecclesiastical student in Paris when the play was written.

The real enigma of *Troilus and Cressida* lies for me in the character of Achilles. If Ulysses, as A. L. Rowse suggests, comes nearer to being the spokesman of Shakespeare's own political philosophy than any other of his characters, Achilles must be the furthest from it. I can see no reason within the play for his making Achilles so peculiarly vile. Indeed, to me he is the vilest character in all of the plays, for he is the only one without a redeeming feature. Edmund and Iago have pluck and humor; Shylock has dignity and passion; Richard III is a superb actor; Aaron loves his baby; Angelo and Iachimo repent; but Achilles is disloyal, dishonest, boastful, at once a coward and a megalomaniac. The scene in which he struts about Hector, speculating aloud in which part of his body he will ultimately strike his fatal blow, is painful to watch, and his conduct at the end where he asks Hector to spare him and then later slaughters him unarmed (doing even this by his Myrmidons and not by his own sword) leaves me asking what is the purpose of this spectacle of human degradation. For Achilles is never amusing and exciting to watch as are the other villains. One feels that Shakespeare must have disliked him too much to let him be attractive, even for a moment. Why?

I believe that the answer must be in some way associated with homosexuality. The relationship between Achilles and Patroclus is the only one in all of the plays that is a homosexual one. Of course it is not so labeled by any character but Thersites, who is more scurrilous than reliable, and it is also true that Achilles is shown as in love with Polyxena and Patroclus as attracted to Cressida, but against these reservations we have the traditional aspect of pederasty in the myth of Achilles and the fact that in ancient Greece a love affair with a youth in no way precluded one with a woman. I think we may take it for a fact that Thersites knows what he is talking about when he calls Patroclus Achilles' "masculine whore." I also take it that the contempt which he proceeds to heap on such "preposterous discoveries" (i.e., masculine whores) is shared by Shakespeare. I see little other reason for putting this speech of Thersites in the play.

There are, of course, other friendships among Shakespeare's men, romantic friendships. There is Antonio in *Twelfth Night* who adores Sebastian and Antonio in *The Merchant of Venice* who will die content if he can but see Bassanio first. There are Proteus and Valentine in

Two Gentlemen of Verona. And, above all, there is the passionate attachment of the poet for the fair youth of the sonnets. But it seems perfectly clear that none of these (with one possible exception in the later sonnets to be examined in a further essay) is a physically homosexual relationship. The famous Sonnet XX underlines this, and in the couplet proclaims what may have been to Shakespeare the vital distinction:

> But since she pricked thee out for women's pleasure,
> Mine be thy love, and thy love's use their treasure.

When Valentine offers to give up Silvia to Proteus, is his action not consistent with this sentiment? The most intense and beautiful emotion in the world, according to the Shakespeare of this period, is that of love between two men, friends not lovers. Physical love is left to women, to dark mistresses, to less noble creatures. I realize that *Romeo and Juliet* and *Othello* will be promptly flung in my face, to which I can only answer that Shakespeare was a poet of many moods and that certainly one of them was informed by this Grecian ideal of friendship. I suspect that he hated Achilles and Patroclus because their relationship seemed to imply that men could not be lovers without being physical lovers or without at least wanting to be. Such would not have been a pleasant concept to one who liked to divorce the spirit and the body in a way that our era does not consider possible. But who knows that we are right?

Coriolanus, the Lonely Dragon

OUR CENTURY has been so harassed with the problem of balancing the equities between the general welfare and the rights of minorities, so plagued with efforts to rebut the fascist and communist theories that social betterment must always be imposed from above, that it is difficult for critics not to see in the conflict between the patrician Coriolanus and the tribunes of the Roman people the theme of a political play. What could seem at first blush more obvious? Coriolanus is the embodiment of ancient aristocracy: high-minded, war-loving, careless of personal gain, conceiving it the natural function of his class to govern the common herd for whose safety it is militarily responsible. Sicinius and Brutus, on the other hand, the popular tribunes, are intent on controlling the state through a manipulated public and tend, like many politicians, to satisfy today at the expense of tomorrow.

And indeed we should have a political theme if we had a true political conflict, if Coriolanus were a rational statesman *seeking* political power and if the tribunes were opposing him simply because he represents his class, if, in other words, it were a case of the nobility against the aroused mob, or even of the nobility against the people. But Coriolanus is not rational. His contempt for the populace is an obsession, deplored by his oldest friend, by his mother and by most of his fellow patricians. There is nothing in the play to indicate that he has the faintest spark of political ambition, and it should have been obvious to the most obtuse Roman noble that he had better be kept as far from the Capitol as possible. To run him for office would be like running Nasser in Israel. When he does run, the tribunes oppose him because his insulting behavior makes it impossible for them politically to do anything else, not because they cannot tolerate an aristocrat in the office of consul.

What brings about this ridiculous situation is not the nomination of Coriolanus for consul by any convention of patricians, but the general feeling in Rome that the military savior of the City must be a consul. Coriolanus is in the position of General Grant in 1868. And his being caught in the trap of national gratitude is the one event that is bound to destroy him, which seems to me the true theme and tragedy of the play. Coriolanus, like Macbeth and Leontes, is the victim of his own obsessions and fantasies, which a trick of fate gives him the unhappy opportunity to act out in reality. Shakespeare, in his later years, was increasingly absorbed with the problem of human perversity: men acting suddenly and irrationally against their own happiness and best interests: Lear dividing his kingdom, Leontes destroying his family, Macbeth ruthlessly and joylessly murdering his own soul. Othello might seem another case in point, yet on closer examination he does not qualify. The others mentioned cling to their perversity; Othello would be overjoyed to catch Iago in a lie. Leontes is so bewitched by his own fantasies that he doubts the validity of the Oracle that he has invoked. Othello would have fallen on his knees before the wronged Desdemona.

The theme of *Coriolanus* is a psychological one that seems to belong more to our post-Freudian world than to Shakespeare's. The protagonist is unique among the tragic heroes of the Jacobean era in that his creator endows him with a childhood and a mother more than adequate to have created the neurosis from which he suffers. Indeed, his story is a capsule case history.

We know very little of the childhood of Shakespeare's other heroes. In fact, we know little of what has happened to them before we see them on stage. If A. C. Bradley has a fault, it is in overelaborating the biographies of the characters, deducing them from the slender facts given. I doubt if Shakespeare ever stopped to consider what Hamlet studied in Wittenberg or whether King Lear's marriage was happy. And all we really know about pre-Act I Macbeth is that he had already considered killing Duncan. But consider what we know about Caius Marcius Coriolanus.

Before he even comes on stage we learn from the "first

citizen" that he has fought his battles to please his mother. Now this citizen is a surly, distrustful type who is not meant to be fully believed, but that a member of the mob should know even this much about Volumnia warns us of the importance of this particular mother-son relationship. And Volumnia, one of Shakespeare's most magnificent creations, tells us all the rest we need to know. She is ludicrous, but she is splendid. In the very second sentence that she utters she states that if Marcius were her husband, she would be happier in his absence on the glorious battlefield than "in the embracements of his bed." Incidentally, this preference of battle to sexual pleasure is echoed by her son who is as merry in victory as when his marriage ceremony was over "and tapers burnt to bedward." Volumnia is pleased to hear that her grandson has mangled a butterfly, and she thanks the gods at the news that her son has been wounded. There is no mention of Marcius' father, which seems quite appropriate; I see Marcius as the posthumous single child (Volumnia describes him as the "only son of my womb") of a fallen hero brought up by this dedicated dragon and sent as a near juvenile to the wars to prove his manhood. It is clear to everyone, including Volumnia, and certainly never disputed by her poor daughter-in-law, that Marcius is his mother's creation.

She has encouraged his pride and his bloodlust; she has infused in him all her own snobbish hatred of the lower classes which he and she attempt to justify by bracketing the occasional cowardice of a foot soldier with the soldier's social origin. To be poor and to be yellow are roughly the same thing to the Marcius clan. But what Volumnia has *not* been able to give to her emotionally crippled, almost hysterically isolated son is her own excellent brain and sense of political expediency, and this failure she at first totally fails to recognize. She quite takes for granted that when Marcius stands for the Consulate he will be able to get through the simple if hypocritical ceremony of asking the people for their voices. She has no conception of how sick a man he is, no idea of what she has done to him. And when, to her horror, she sees the ghastly mess that he makes of the whole business, she turns on him:

> O, sir, sir, sir,
> I would have had you put your power well on
> Before you had worn it out.

Shakespeare understood that the great strength of such mothers as Volumnia is that they can never conceive that anything could be their fault. They take full credit for the assets and slough off the liabilities:

> Thy valiantness was mine, thou suckedst it from me;
> But owe thy pride thyself.

However, she does at last take in that Marcius cannot extricate himself from his own predicament without her help, and she moves in, as she must have done in his younger days, to take control:

I prithee now, sweet son, as thou hast said
My praises made thee first a soldier, so,
To have my praise for this, perform a part
Thou hast not done before.

She counsels him well and astutely, comparing the necessary hypocrisy of the politician to the soldier's strategic deception in surprising an enemy town, but, of course, nothing can help Marcius now. He is at the mercy of the first man who taunts him, and the tribunes, who know his fiery compulsions, have him in their hands.

The climax of Marcius' egomania comes in the great explosive speech when he retorts to his banishers. Here he releases himself with a kind of exultation to his frenzy; he becomes Rome itself, the real Rome, and banishes the population who are unworthy to be Romans. He is obviously a child again, a boy of dreams, and like a little boy, taking leave of his family in the following scene, he hopes that his mother has approved of his proud act and is surprised by her drooping spirits. But Volumnia has finally seen what he is; she knows now that the case is hopeless. She is not in the least moved by his project to roam the world as a "lonely dragon" and begs him to take Cominius with him as a tutor to save him from a "wild exposure" to each chance.

There is nothing further now that she can do until Marcius appears before the gates of Rome at the head of an army of his old enemies and threatens to sack the city. Then in a final application of her maternal dominion, she makes him give up his revenge at the cost of his life. It is not clear that she knows that his renunciation will be fatal to him, as she does not speak again after Marcius tells her that she has prevailed "most dangerously" for him, but I do not doubt that for as fierce a patriot as Volumnia, who loved to inspect her son's wounds, the choice between him and her country would be a simple, if not automatic one.

I wonder if Shakespeare intended the irony of the little scene, only seven lines in length, that immediately precedes that of Marcius' death. Volumnia passes in triumph over the stage, invoked as "our patroness, the life of Rome," to a flourish of drums and trumpets, while off in Antium her son falls the victim of the sacrifice she has demanded of him. It is not enough that he must owe his courage to his mother. In the end she will take his life and steal his victory! Swinburne said that the inscription on the plinth of the tragic statue should be "Volumnia Victrix."

I believe that Coriolanus' contempt for popular rule may have been a deliberate exaggeration of something that Shakespeare felt within himself. Again and again in the plays he sides with order, precedence, degree, what we would call the "establishment." He was not a believer in the divine right of kings, but very possibly in the divine right of kingship. He finds it wrong, for example, to depose a king, but right to obey an established usurper. It seems to boil down to a preference for a questionable status quo over the tumult of civil disobedience. But seeing all around a question as Shakespeare always did, he could see himself, even satirically, as a conservative, and it may have been a part of his art to put his own opinions on the stage in caricature. Coriolanus is exaggerated in everything, even in vanity. He praises himself indirectly when he denigrates the qualities he lacks. Because he is good for nothing outside the battlefield, because aside from his bravery he has nothing but his birth, he must always be blasting cowardice and low social station. This is the mechanism by which he constantly protects himself from self-doubts.

It is the note that he strikes in his very first appearance. He seems to welcome the riots for the opportunity that they afford him to speak out: "What would you have, you curs, that like not peace or war?"

I do not see how one can mistake the psychological as opposed to political structure of the tragedy in this outburst:

> Would the nobility lay aside their ruth
> And let me use my sword, I'd make a quarry
> With thousands of these quartered slaves, as high
> As I could pick my lance.

Some candidate!

Coriolanus makes only a token effort to comply with the ancient custom of soliciting voices and blows up at the first taunt thereafter. The patricians bring in Volumnia who is only able to get him to the Forum and there he blows up again. I cannot read into this scene a man standing up for a principle against a mob. It is a deep need of Coriolanus' emotionally seething nature to expectorate in the face of the people. Having done so he faces exile with an almost philosophical calm. But he has his plan already, and it consoles him for the misery of his parting.

The tragedy now moves on to Coriolanus' unique opportunity and consequent unique suffering. He has the chance that very few psychotics have: to translate into reality his fantasies of revenge. To lead the enemy against his native city and put his sword to the necks of the offensive tribunes, to prove that all along he was *right*, that they could not subsist without his strong right arm — is it not a dream? Who has not imagined that kind of victory over a parent, a headmaster, a commanding officer, a boss? The remarkable power of the play is in the way it fills the reader's heart with the cloudy exultation of the marching nemesis, bringing a terrible justice and a total self-justification.

And then comes the deadening scene of misery of Act V when Coriolanus sees that his revenge is nothing but his suicide, that he has overturned a lifetime of valor to strike a blow at his own home. I think he is actually relieved when Volumnia comes out to dot every last "i" of his insurrection and cross every "t" of his treachery. She is mother again, the stern mother of his childhood, and he must stop playing games. The game has become scary, anyway; it is no longer fun. He is glad to have the excuse of his filial duty to turn back to Antium.

There he finds his old fantasy again and dies in something like the happiness of his frenzy. All that is familiar at least; it is not the hell of seeing Rome under his treacherous sword. Once again he is manipulated, as he was manipulated by the tribunes. All Aufidius has to do is to insult him by calling him "boy," and he ensures his own assassination by shouting insults at the Volscians:

> Boy! False Hound!
> If you have writ your annals true, 'tis there,
> That like an eagle in a dovecote, I
> Fluttered your Volscians in Corioli
> Alone I did it — Boy!

It is only the logical last step of his long suicide.

Caesar, the Tudor Monarch

JULIUS CAESAR, like *Coriolanus*, is generally considered a political play. But it seems to me to deal almost exclusively with the theme of assassination. In the last century and in our own, American and English critics have tended to see it as a balanced conflict between the virtues of killing an incipient tyrant and the dangers of disrupting society with a consequent civil war. Many readers go further and find the scales tipped in Brutus' favor; he is the hero and Caesar a Hitler or Mussolini. One remembers the famous Orson Welles production of the play in which Caesar was actually represented as a Nazi. But I find no justification for either theory in the text.

To begin with, it is not one hundred percent clear that Caesar was actually seeking the crown, although Plutarch, the source, says he was, and the fact that he yields to Decius' persuasion to go to the Senate is probably based on Decius' hint that the Senate has in mind to make him such an offer. Yet Caesar, unlike other Shakespearean characters who suffer from ambition, never says he wants the crown. But even if he did, would it seem so wicked to an Englishman, living under the rule of Elizabeth, that a man already at the helm of state should seek to be King? We know from the historical plays that Shakespeare thought it wrong to usurp a crown, but Caesar would not have been usurping one. What the Senate planned to offer him was only the outward and visible form of a power he already enjoyed.

It has also been argued that Caesar is shown in the play as an arrogant and unyielding man who has the soul of a despot and who could reasonably be expected to trample any remaining liberties of the Romans under his feet. Of course, the pomposity of Caesar's speeches offers some support for this, but I doubt that Shakespeare intended Caesar to be as pompous as his part reads to a twentieth-century eye. It is true that he sometimes speaks of himself in the third person, which has a grandiloquent ring in a nonmonarch, but he is the undoubted ruler of a great empire, and Shakespeare may have considered this form of expression perfectly fitting. He allows many rulers in his plays to take themselves very seriously indeed without seeming to denigrate them. What seems pompous to us, accustomed as we are to the compulsive humility of our own political candidates, may have appeared to Elizabethans as the gravity and majesty expected of a chief of state.

As to Caesar's being unyielding, as he shows himself in

refusing to pardon the exiled Publius Cimber, he may be being merely just, and there are many incidents in Shakespeare's plays where rigorous rulers are regarded as only doing their job. Nowhere in the play does Caesar speak of suppressing liberties, nor is he ever shown doing it except for the two tribunes who are "put to silence" (which apparently does *not* mean capital punishment) for pulling scarves off his images.

On the positive side of Caesar's character, we note that he has inspired the total loyalty of Marc Antony. I see no reason to disbelieve the compliments conferred upon him in Antony's funeral oration. Caesar's death is followed by a civil war in which Shakespeare must have seen a parallel to the Wars of the Roses that had so obsessed his earlier years. Certainly we know that Shakespeare stood for civil order above everything, and Caesar's death was followed by the destruction of the existing order.

Finally, there is the matter of Caesar's ghost. We do not tend to take ghosts very seriously today, but Shakespeare's audience did. Caesar's ghost was Caesar's ghost, and if he appeared to haunt his murderer, it was because his murderer had done a wicked thing in killing him.

Turning now to the conspirators, it is very plain that they are all motivated by selfish reasons with the sole exception of Brutus. They have brought Brutus into their camp only to lend respectability to a cause that would otherwise lack it. This, it seems to me, brings us to the real subject of the tragedy: that of a man who is persuaded to commit an assassination for high motives, but an assassination which no high motives could justify.

To me the most startling scene of the play is that where Antony, Lepidus and Octavius Caesar are first shown together. The drama of tears and funeral praises is over; now these three are getting down to the business of revenge and dividing the spoils. There is even a hint that they are deflecting the money in Caesar's estate from the people to their own uses. It is all the more effective for our having last seen Marc Antony at the height of his eloquence, but I am not entirely sure of its purpose. Possibly Shakespeare is showing yet another evil effect of the assassination. Not only has it broken the State into warring parties, but the party that will prevail is already at odds within itself.

The fact that Marc Antony seems cruel and heartless in condemning his nephew with the prick of a pen does not seem to me, as it does to some commentators, to turn his whole character into that of a cynical politician whose funeral oration has been nothing but a deliberate piece of demagoguery. I believe that his grief at Caesar's death is quite sincere and that his desire for revenge is motivated more by his regret for Caesar than by personal ambition. It may not be stretching things too far to see in the immediate degeneration of Marc Antony, the loyal hound, into Marc Antony, the cynical seeker of world power, still another fatal consequence of Brutus' crime.

Caesar's statements about Cassius and his distrust of thin men are frequently read as the mutterings of a dictator who cannot abide the least independence of thought. But Caesar has every justification for distrusting Cassius, who is already plotting his murder, and he puts his finger on Cassius' primary motive, which is simple envy. In further evidence that Caesar has not been a tyrant, I cite Brutus' startling admission that Caesar is not and has never been a tyrant. Brutus is frank to state that his entire motivation lies in his fear that Caesar *may* become a tyrant, given the opportunity that the crown will give him. Now some modern readers may think that this kind of preventive assassination is justified in the interests of freedom and assume that Shakespeare is of their point of view. But I repeat that Caesar was already a dictatorial ruler in the Tudor sense, with a good record for justice at the opening of the play, and I do not think that his coronation could have been regarded by an Elizabethan as the automatic transformation of a benevolent despot into a tyrant.

Mary McCarthy has said that the play is the tragedy of an idealist forced into action, with the implication that possibly all action is bad. I would amend this by saying that the play is the tragedy of an idealist persuaded to assassination and that all assassination is bad. Shakespeare was a man of his time and believed in strong monarchs like the Tudors. That he never quite makes them palatable to readers raised in a different political theory does not mean that he did not intend to. Julius Caesar belongs in the category of Vincentio, Prospero and Henry V.

Bertram, the Cad Hero

THERE HAS ALWAYS been concern among some commentators over the flawed characters of some of Shakespeare's comedy heroes. Valentine in *Two Gentlemen of Verona* offers to give up Silvia to his friend Proteus whom he has just forcibly restrained from raping her; Bassanio in *The Merchant of Venice* is frankly interested in Portia's money; Posthumus (for I cannot accept *Cymbeline* as a tragedy) dispatches Iachimo to the English Court with letters of recommendation that he may have ample opportunity to test Imogen's virtue; and Demetrius and Lysander in *A Midsummer Night's Dream* treat Helena and Hermia with shocking rudeness. Claudio, worse yet, in *Much Ado about Nothing,* instead of withdrawing discreetly from what he has been made to consider a dishonorable match, brings his betrothed to the altar that he may publicly humiliate her. But from Dr. Johnson's day to our own, it is Bertram in *All's Well that Ends Well* who receives the crown for caddishness.

His bad reputation in the last century carried over to

besmirch Helena a bit. Without him she would have been one of Shakespeare's most popular heroines, one of the finest of those eloquent, high-minded, noble-hearted women who are so frank about their hearts' commitments and have such partiality for male attire. But Helena distressed Victorian readers by her indelicate joking with Parolles on the subject of virginity and by the gross trick that she employed to ensnare her husband. It was bad enough for a lady to push, but far worse to push for so worthless a spouse.

Summing up the case against Bertram, it does seem at first blush a bad one. Even if we sympathize with his chagrin at having a wife of lower birth imposed upon him by royal fiat, he is certainly nasty to send her home with so vindictive a letter, and he is repellently heartless at the report of her death. He is a fool to be taken in by Parolles and a bad sport when he catches him out; he cannot understand the tolerance of the amused Captain Dumain who, hearing himself outrageously abused by the blindfolded and hoodwinked rascal, merely says "I begin to love him for this." On leaving the supposedly seduced Diana, Bertram is only afraid of future consequences to himself, and, asked by the King where he got Helena's ring, he tells an elaborate lie. When Diana appears to refute this, he accuses her of being a "common gamester to the camp." For all of this behavior, as Doctor Johnson puts it, he is "dismissed to happiness."

But I think to our day, as to the Elizabethans, Bertram

appears in a different light. We are franker than the Victorians in recognizing the brutal, pugnacious, strutting attitude of young males in the first pride of their virility. We even admire it. Marlon Brando has been worshipped on stage and screen for his portrayal of somber, ruttish youths. We understand their attraction for women of keener minds and finer sensibilities. That Helena should be captivated by Bertram's beauty, that her love should be intensified by his very brutality and infidelity, is easy enough for us to imagine. That she will do anything to get into his bed, even in the guise of another woman, and thoroughly enjoy herself there, as she frankly states, without a vestige of romantic love on his part, makes for our diversion. Indeed, I think we, like the Elizabethans, find the "bed trick" rather sexy. If one refuses to concede that the play is about a superior woman, trapped in the strait-jacket of her physical passion and determined at any cost to mate with a rather ordinary (except in battle) young man, the drama becomes shapeless and pointless. But following the theme as I have put it, the play can be alive and moving.

Helena is ashamed of the violence and social impropriety of her passion. In her first soliloquy she admits that the image of Bertram has obliterated that of her recently deceased father. When Parolles greets her with the crude question: "Are you meditating on virginity?," it is exactly what she is doing. It is an actual relief to her to join in his dirty jokes. Her infatuation is so obvious that everyone suspects it; she talks aloud of it, is overheard, and blurts it all out to the Countess at the first opportunity. Then she hurries off to Paris with her desperate plan, risking her very life for the chance to purchase Bertram. Not for a minute does she blame him for his resentment of this. She is at all times perfectly fair. But she will not give up, nor will she criticize Bertram for his attempted seduction of Diana. She is simply grateful for the second chance it affords her. And when she gets her man in the end, the smallness of her victory is perhaps unintentionally expressed by the poet's failure of inspiration in Bertram's final couplet:

> If she, my Liege, can make me know this clearly,
> I'll love her dearly, ever, ever dearly.

But Helena perhaps has not done so badly, after all. Bertram has beauty, breeding and physical courage, and he is shown as very young. He is "in ward" to the King, which implies that he is still a minor. Is it so unusual for young soldiers to be selfish, proud, stubborn and lustful? Bertram should be played by an actor whose boyish good looks immediately predispose an audience in his favor. We must see at once why Helena is content to sit and draw in her heart's table "his arched brows, his hawking eye, his curls." And what is more humiliating for a young gallant who has just made his first appearance at court than to be ordered by the King to marry a family retainer? I think he shows a good deal of pluck in going as far as he does in attempting to defy his monarch; the other courtiers, be it noticed, have evidenced an immediate submission in the matter of wedding where royal favor inclines.

Coming to Florence and his meanness about Parolles — his desire to have him whipped through the camp — it must be remembered that Bertram is the only one in the plot who has been personally humiliated by Parolles. He alone, because of his youth and inexperience, has trusted him. And when the King asks where he got Helena's ring, it is understandable that he is reluctant to tell the group, including his own future father-in-law, that it was given him in bed. When Diana comes in and demands that he marry her, any last obligation that he may think he owes her is forfeited, and he assumes what any man under such circumstances would assume: that she is a hussy who is trying to capture a titled husband. It is only to be expected that he will treat her as a prostitute.

After all, this is the second time that poor Bertram has been claimed in marriage, of the King, before a crowd of courtiers, by a woman he does not love! It is enough to make any man brutal.

Time has even taught me a certain tolerance of Claudio in *Much Ado about Nothing*. There the real hero is Benedick (we know that Charles I reentitled the play *Beatrice and Benedick* in his second folio), so it is dramatically permissible to bespeckle the character of the *jeune premier*. Actually, it makes Claudio more interesting. He is a brave fighter but a spoiled and peevish brat.

He is too shy to undertake his own wooing of Hero and too quickly jealous of Don Pedro who undertakes it for him. His public disgrace of his bride is unmanly, and his callousness to her stricken father and uncle in the street is unspeakable. But he rallies handsomely when he finds that he is in the wrong, and he very properly offers to make amends by marrying Hero's cousin, though he need not have added "were she an Ethiope." And I like his willingness to make up with Benedick. I feel that there is hope for Claudio's recovery in the future when he swallows the latter's final quip:

> Bull Jove, sir, had an amiable low;
> And some such strange bull leapt your father's cow,
> And got a calf in that same noble feat,
> Much like to you, for you have just his bleat.

Shakespeare saw no reason that his young heroes should not be as other young men.

The Enigma of Measure for Measure

I SUPPOSE THAT there is more variety among the interpretations of *Measure for Measure* than any other play of Shakespeare's except *Hamlet*. With which characters does the author intend to engage our sympathies? With any? How are we meant to react to the edict against fornication? Has Claudio really sinned at all by living with his bride after a legal betrothal? Is Isabella supposed to be punished in the last act? Is the Duke meant to be God?

It is amusing to see how violent some of the commentators become about these characters. I have seen the Duke described as a heartless and capricious prig, Isabella as an hysterical puritan and Claudio as a dishonorable coward. But it is about Isabella and the Duke that the principal discord rages. Isabella's champions maintain that she is splendid throughout or, if she is a trifle at fault in her pride, that she learns humility in the end. The Duke's champions see him very much as he sees himself: as a wise and infinitely conscientious ruler, who can hardly sleep in his concern over his realm.

This kind of discord over fundamental aspects of character is rare in Shakespearean criticism. It seems to me evident, from the conclusion of the play in the betrothal of the Duke and Isabella and the simultaneous return of justice to the troubled duchy, that Shakespeare must have intended to show some approval of them. Yet it is also undeniable that throughout the play he invites our attention to their least lovable characteristics. I think that a survey of these invitations may be illuminating.

Let us start with Isabella. We see her, at the very outset, criticizing the vows of the convent (which she is about to take) as too lax. She wishes "a more strict restraint upon the sisterhood." When, persuaded by Lucio, she goes to Angelo to plead for her brother's life, she is perfectly willing to give it all up at the first rebuff. "O just but severe law!" she exclaims; "I *had* a brother, then," and proceeds at once to take her leave of Angelo. Lucio has to push her back, pointing out that if she should need a pin, she could not "with more tame a tongue desire it." It is interesting to note that in her later scene with Claudio she unconsciously echoes this idea. She tells him that she would gladly give up her life for him — which nobody has requested of her. Oh, yes, if it were only *that* which Angelo wanted and not her chaste treasure, she would throw it down for her brother's deliverance "as frankly as a pin." Claudio's laconic response: "Thanks, dear Isabel," should always get a big laugh in a theater. For if Isabella, like Hamlet, does not value her life "at a pin's fee," it is clear that she values her brother's no higher.

At this point I begin to have a clue. Isabella is being used as a butt. She can be enormously funny, played correctly, from her very first speech about the "more strict restraint." But she must never lose her dignity because she has the splendid mercy speech that is more eloquent even than Portia's. Isabella's role requires considerable subtlety from an actress.

On her second interview with Angelo, she accepts a second rebuff as quickly as her first. She starts to walk out again, but this time Angelo himself, Lucio being absent, has to stop her. So mild is her zeal that the judge denying her plea must beg her to plead again! When Claudio's timorous behavior gives her the excuse she needs to wash her hands of the whole dirty business, she lashes the poor man with an angry tongue, telling him that mercy to him would be a bawd:

> Might but my bending down
> Reprieve thee from thy fate, it should proceed.

Hurrying from Claudio's cell she meets the disguised Duke who begs a word with her. She cuts him off at once, saying that she has no "superfluous leisure," that any stay must be stolen out of other affairs. She is scurrying back to the all-consuming business of saving her own soul. When the Duke tells her of Mariana's desertion by Angelo, she expresses her sympathy, quite simply, by wishing Mariana an early death. That is her solution to everything: early death and quick salvation. When the Duke attempts to console her for Claudio's supposed death, he finds her quickly resigned. He hardly need tell her to reflect that Claudio is happier dead than living: "I do, my lord" is her prompt reply. To maintain, with some commentators, that she atones for her pride is to write a new last act. After a single brief moment of embarrassment, she is made Duchess of Vienna.

Consider now the evolution of the Duke's character. He begins by subjecting the hitherto virtuous Angelo to a test which he suspects will bring out the worst in him. His purpose in doing this is twofold: he will uncover an unworthy public servant, and he will place the onus of the enforcement of hitherto unenforced laws on shoulders other than his own. But is there any reason to suppose that Angelo, free of the temptations of executive authority, would not have continued a reliable officer? And can it be admirable for a statesman to let inferiors be his scapegoats? The Duke is very free with other people's feelings. He allows Juliet to believe that Claudio will die; he allows Claudio to believe that Claudio will die; and, even less justifiably, for she has done no wrong, even by his strict code, he allows Isabella to believe that Claudio is dead. He gives Claudio a long sermon on the horrors of life and the blessings of death in which neither he nor Claudio really believe, for he intends all the while to remit Claudio's sentence, and Claudio immediately afterward begs his sister to save his life at the price of her honor. He berates Pompey with undue violence, foreshadowing Prospero's impatience with Caliban, and he is absurdly put out of countenance by Lucio.

How I love Lucio! All my pent-up irritations at the Duke's complacent and artificial interference in the lives of his poor subjects bursts out in the scenes where he abuses the Duke. I clap my hands as Lucio strikes him with one magnificent slander after another, all the more effective for being such slanders and hopeless to rebut. It provides a kind of comic catharsis, comparable to the relief we feel in *Othello* when Emilia defies the Moor and cries that her dead mistress was "too fond of her most filthy bargain." No matter how well-meaning the Duke, no matter how deceived Othello, it is time these things were said.

Now, obviously, if the Duke is to be considered an ordinary mortal, he is insufferable. He cannot, on the other hand, be God, as some critics have surmised, for this would have been sacrilegious in Shakespeare's day, and besides, if the Duke were God he could not be deceived into believing that Angelo means to pardon Claudio after accepting Isabella's bribe, nor would he be frustrated in his plan for Barnardine. Shakespeare, I think, must have intended to make the Duke the exemplar of a Tudor monarch. He always allowed his monarchs to be more sententious and less humorous than other people, as befits their vast responsibilities.

If, then, Shakespeare intended the Duke to be an admirable monarch and saw Isabella as a fitting spouse for him, why does he make such fun of them? I suggest that his story got out of hand. The play is supposed to deal with the relationship of statesmanship and mercy, a very serious theme. But Shakespeare made an unfortunate choice in his selection of the law whose vigorous enforcement was to provide the arena of discussion. This law would have been as unthinkable in the London of 1604 as in London today. Leniency in its respect would not have been an act of mercy but of political necessity. No society has ever been able to legislate effectively against fornication — let alone fornication between a man and woman legally betrothed and anxious to marry. A Jacobean audience would know as well as a modern one that the remission of Claudio's penalty was a simple act of justice. To confuse it with mercy is to introduce absurdity into the play.

Having introduced it, however, Shakespeare could only save the situation by taking some of the absurdity of the law and scattering it over its proponents. This enables the audience to laugh at the statute and at its would-be enforcers rather than wax indignant or impatient with them. Isabella harps too much on her virginity; she becomes self-righteous. The Duke is too lofty in his standards for his subjects, too impatient of vice; he needs Lucio to take him down. The foolishness of the legal situation is concealed in the satire.

By bringing the anti-vice characters to a near draw with the pro-vice characters, by allowing Lucio to greet Isabella with "Hail, Virgin, if you be" and to tell the supposed Friar that the Duke was "a very superficial, ignorant, unweighing fellow" who would "mouth with a beggar, though she smelt brown bread and garlic," by making the good prudish and the foul rather lovably droll, Shakespeare is able now to pick his almost lost serious theme out of the character of Angelo. For Angelo's wickedness exists quite apart from the fornication statute. It is not the statute that is really important here, but that he has condemned a man to death for what he would do himself. Once he has thrust this bar to his conscience aside, he knows no more restraints. He is a liberated sadist who can threaten Claudio with torture as well as decapitation and find an added titillation in the very horror which he arouses in Isabella. Angelo's wickedness fits perfectly into the plot. There is no need to make *him* funny.

Why, then, did Shakespeare make use of the fornication law? Why, when he found that he was running into trouble, did he not alter it? A hundred other equally unjust but less unusual statutes could be thought of. Well, in the first place the law was in the source, Whetstone's play *Promos and Cassandra*, and Shakespeare was inclined to be faithful to the main outlines of his sources. He changed the story by preserving Isabella's virtue, but this was not as basic to the old plot as the bizarre statute. And secondly, the statute offered rich comic opportunities for the type of bawdry that Shakespeare loved: he could fill his stage with lechers and pimps and make rare humor out of their outrage at the sudden thunder of puritanism in old Vienna.

And, finally, there is the possibility that he knew precisely what he was doing from the beginning: that all along he had planned a situation where a ludicrous law and its savage enforcement would satirize the attempt of a small minority to control the beast in man. Under this view we are given a picture of Pompey, Lucio, Mistress Overdone, the Clown and Froth, the world of the brothel, as the *real* world, or at least as the world of the vast majority, while on the other side we see the pathetic little self-important group of would-be rulers, the officious Duke, the sadist Angelo, the hysterical virgin Isabella, trying to write their names on a boiling ocean of lust and lechery. It is a tempting interpretation, but I do not really believe that Shakespeare intended it. He was too much on the Duke's side.

There are so many denunciations of sexual looseness in Shakespeare's later work, commencing with *Troilus and Cressida* and running right through to *Pericles*, that it is difficult not to speculate that he was a conservative in morals as well as politics. The fact that he himself (if the Sonnets are autobiographical) had a "dark mistress" as well as a conveniently absent wife would not in the least derogate from this conclusion. In fact, a sense of guilt may have been the origin of his censoriousness. I do not suggest that he would have ever proposed capital punishment for sexual transgression, but he probably believed that the sexual morals of the public should be of prime concern to any ruler, and he very likely sympathized with the Duke's interest in wiping out procurement and prostitution in Vienna.

As a realist, however, he knew that it could never be done. And with that extraordinary fairness that makes him unique among writers he made his bawds and pimps as sympathetic — perhaps more sympathetic — than the principal characters of whose rather brassy virtues he may have more basically approved.

Shakespeare and Royalty

It is not my purpose to waste any time here on attempted rebuttals of crackpot theories about the authorship of Shakespeare's plays. It is impossible to rebut a speculation based on pure hypothesis. Duff Cooper put it well in his *Sergeant Shakespeare* when he pointed out that it should be necessary, before showing that somebody else wrote Shakespeare's works, to prove first that he did not write them himself. Nobody has ever done this. But there is one argument used over and over by the "anti-Stratford" enthusiasts (whichever nobleman their candidate happens to be) that strikes me as peculiarly idiotic, and that is that Shakespeare's plays must have been written by a person born close to the crown because of the intimate familiarity that they show with court life.

The middle and later middle plays do indeed show that their author knew something of the "great world" of London, but by then he had appeared before the Queen herself on numerous occasions and had probably prepared performances for some of the great private houses. Who is quicker than an actor in picking up the essence of any new atmosphere? There is a legend that Shakespeare received the personal favor of James I, which would have given him the chance to study power at its very font, but there is nothing whatever in the early work to suggest the smallest acquaintance with royal circles. In fact the very reverse is true. The young Shakespeare, in this respect, shows himself a bit of a hick.

In *Henry VI, Part II,* Queen Margaret behaves in a most unregal fashion. Not only does she strike her husband's aunt, the Duchess of Gloucester, but she walks on stage behind the King, in the presence of courtiers, bearing the Duke of Suffolk's severed head in her arms and addressing it in loving terms. In *King John* Queen Elinor and her daughter-in-law, Constance, rail at each other like fishwives, and Cardinal Pandulphu, the papal legate, hurries on and off the battlefields to direct the French and English monarchs to fight or not to fight like an umpire with a whistle. In *Henry IV, Part II* the King takes his crown off before retiring and puts it on the table by his bed. Edward IV's wooing of Lady Grey in *Henry VI, Part III* is ludicrous, and the ensuing scene in the Court of France, when the royal audience of Warwick is broken up by the arrival of the mailman, who distributes letters which are immediately opened and read by King and courtiers, borders on farce. Richard II, I admit, has a certain kingliness, but it is of a stagy sort, and Henry V is a pageant monarch.

But if Shakespeare so far showed little firsthand knowledge of life at court, he was already developing his ideas on sovereignty. *Richard II* is evidence of this. Shakespeare had an almost religious sense of the inviolability of the crown, and he represents the Wars of the Roses and the loss of France as a nemesis following the usurpation of the throne by the House of Lancaster. All the prayers and good deeds of Henry IV, all the military triumphs of Henry V, cannot atone for the deposition and murder of Richard. That crime must be revenged in the endless disasters of the reign of Henry VI and in the murders by which Richard III hacks his way to the crown. Not until the latter has perished, bellowing for a horse, can peace return to Britain with the reconciliation of Lancaster and York in the House of Tudor.

Richard II has caused some confusion in our century because of our interest in the qualities of self-pity and self-dramatization which the King shows in the last three acts. His inability to cope with reality and his seemingly deliberate effort to rescue himself from the degradation of defeat by the wings of his own poetry, by his own splendid dramatization of the role of deposed King, are of absorbing interest to post-Freudian generations. But I have always been uneasy about attributing self-pity to Elizabethan characters who lament their fate in what may have been simply a literary fashion. One does not have to read very far in Elizabethan literature to realize that characters bewail their own tragedies at very great length without necessarily incurring the blame of self-pity. Witness

Constance in *King John*, whose woes are obviously not of her own making but who is nonetheless accused by King Philip of being as fond of grief as of her abducted child, just as Richard is accused by Bolingbroke of playing with shadows. Yet Shakespeare's sympathy is obviously with Constance.

In the first two acts of *Richard II* the King never rises to the eloquence that he shows when he arrives on the coast of Wales and weeps for joy to stand upon his kingdom again. The early scenes are devoted to building up the case against him. He behaves arbitrarily at the lists at Coventry, stopping the duel between Bolingbroke and Norfolk at the last moment and banishing them both. We learn that he has been responsible for the murder of his uncle Gloucester and that he has beggared the kingdom by leasing out crown lands. He has given unlimited power to his dissipated intimates, and he is brutally rude to old John of Gaunt when the latter offers his dying counsel to save him in his downward course. So far Richard is without a redeeming trait.

It is clearly, however, Shakespeare's thesis that nothing can justify the deposition of a monarch. Even if it results in the temporary alleviation of wrongs committed by a tyrant, seizure of the crown must always be paid in bloodshed which in the long run will offset any immediate benefits. As Richard goes to his fall, his language rises to heights of beauty, particularly where it deals with the spiritual powers of the crown. The more it becomes apparent that Bolingbroke and his forces have occupied every avenue of power, the more does Richard, in his isolation and tragedy, achieve a truly royal dignity. In the deposition scene he thoroughly dominates the stage and makes Bolingbroke seem a sordid intruder. To me his lines in the last acts are more prophetic than self-pitying. I believe they are designed to irradiate the English background with a sense of the splendor of the crown and of the enormity of the crime that has eclipsed it. For this crime must be expiated not only in the plays that Shakespeare was about to write, but in the four plays that he had already written, ending in the final union of the Houses of York and Lancaster and the rise of the Tudors to reunite England.

The success of the Lord Chamberlain's company and Shakespeare's now frequent opportunities to see the old Queen in person must have altered his view drastically of what went on in palaces. He probably had opportunities to talk with many of the courtiers. Would it not be natural for at least some of them to want to discuss the plays with the playwright? Can one imagine not wanting to meet the author of *Hamlet?* Legend has it that he was a houseguest at Wilton, that Queen Elizabeth requested that he write *The Merry Wives of Windsor* and that James I, with his own hand, was pleased to write him an "amicable letter." I see nothing unlikely in any of these stories.

In the early historical plays his kings do more fighting

than ruling. In fact they do little else but fight, for when they can no longer fight, like Richard II, they fall. But Queen Elizabeth certainly did no fighting herself, and she sent her soldiers to do so only with the greatest reluctance. Yet she and old Burleigh ruled England with a competence that Shakespeare must have to some extent recognized. Even Polonius in *Hamlet*, tedious old bore that he is and, according to some enthusiastic historical critics, a parody of Burleigh, has some of the characteristics of a statesman. And in Claudius, Polonius' sovereign, we meet with Shakespeare's first real king.

He is one of the poet's rare rational villains. We understand his every motivation, from first to last. He has no prejudices and no compulsions; he commits the minimum number of crimes, in Machiavellian fashion, in order to obtain what he wants: the crown and Gertrude, particularly the crown. I never feel that Claudius has much passion for the Queen; I suspect she is merely a rung in his ladder. But the point about Claudius is that he is an eminently practical man. He knows that his conscience is going to play hell with him, but he also knows that it is going to be worth it. He will be King, which is what he feels he has to be, with all the satisfactions and trappings of power — and with some bad moments. But the good moments will be more than the bad. It is a simple case of making omelets and breaking eggs. And so, indeed, it might have worked out, had it not been for Hamlet. Who could predict a blabbing ghost?

Furthermore, Claudius seems to be a perfectly adequate king. He is pompous and long-winded, to be sure, but this is in accordance with royal tradition. Courtiers may even expect and like it. He handles Hamlet very astutely, putting him in the wrong for his excessive mourning, and he avoids war with Fortinbras by timely negotiations. He does not make any move against Hamlet's life until he has to — there is nothing of Aaron's or Iago's cruelty in Claudius — and when faced with Laertes' riotous mob, he regains control of the situation by the sheer force of personality:

> Let him go, Gertrude; do not fear our person:
> There's such divinity doth hedge a king
> That treason can but peep to what it would,
> Acts little of his will.

Do we not hear Richard II in this, a strong Richard, if such can be imagined? Might it not be Elizabeth herself in the Essex uprising? Had Claudius come legally to the throne, he might, like Hamlet, have proved "most royally," but he has obtained the crown by murder, and all such must come to sorry ends in the Shakespeare canon, with the possible exception of Henry IV, and even he has a pretty bad time of it.

Shakespeare, in this later middle period, was fascinated by the question of power and its exercise. In the elaborate self-discipline of Duke Vincentio in *Measure for Measure*, in the shrewd counsels of Ulysses in *Troilus and Cressida*, in the doubts of Lear about his relief of poverty, in the cold calculations of Octavius Caesar in *Antony and Cleopatra,* we see a far more sophisticated interest in the problems besetting a ruler than in the rather banal assessments of royal responsibility uttered by Henry IV and Henry V. The monarchs of the earlier historical plays seem, in contrast, like princes in a medieval book of hours, simple, naive, posed. Whatever else Claudius may be, he is indubitably King of Denmark.

Yet in conflict with Shakespeare's growing understanding of how difficult it was to be a merciful and at the same time an effective sovereign in late Elizabethan and early Jacobean England, in conflict, too, with his evident admiration of tough, disciplined administrators, like Vincentio and ultimately Prospero, there was always his romantic idea of kings and queens, never quite lost from the early chronicle plays, perhaps originally inspired by Marlowe. That is one of the delights about him. He did not have to face up to every contradiction, every implication in his thinking. He could put things in as he felt them. This may have been what Keats called his "negative capability."

In *King Lear* and in *Antony and Cleopatra* he created a king and a queen who, had he written nothing else, and written them anonymously, might almost seem to justify the supposition that the author was an intimate of royalty. Surely Lear, as he says of himself, is every inch a king, and Cleopatra is royal to the tips of her fingers. Compare the scenes where Queen Margaret strikes the

Duchess of Gloucester and where Cleopatra attacks the messenger bringing the news of Antony's marriage. It is the difference between a schoolgirl and an empress. Shakespeare's royalty, at the height of his writing, are most royal in defeat, even in defeat brought on by their own incompetence. Surely Lear is not modeled on James I, or Cleopatra on Elizabeth, but the man who created them had seen persons of great style at close quarters.

In the fanciful atmosphere of the final plays, the sad romances, we are removed from seventeenth century England to the fairyland atmosphere of a romantically conceived Sicily or Bohemia, to ancient Rome and to legendary Mediterranean kingdoms. There is no longer any need for the wily and practical monarchs of Jacobean times, and we find in these plays a curious return to the quixotic, despotic sovereigns of the early historical chronicle plays.

Cymbeline, for example, is a weak, petulant old man, utterly dependent on his wicked wife and lout of a stepson, incapable of a truly generous thought, even in his own best interests. He makes Lear at his most foolish seem like a tower of strength. Leontes and Polixenes in *The Winter's Tale* behave like madmen, and Antonio and Sebastian in *The Tempest* are villains of melodrama. None of these princes except Prospero show any of the attributes of the more powerful and more true-to-life rulers of the plays of the middle period.

But the curious thing about Shakespeare's depiction of

royalty in these last plays is the return, even more strongly, of the vein of mystic reverence for royal blood that we have noted in *Richard II* and *Henry V*. The two sons of Cymbeline, although brought up in the wilderness without any knowledge of their true birth, turn out bright and brave and true, not, as might be imagined, because of their austere and disciplined education, but because of their royal blood which is bound to show itself despite anything that environment can do. Similarly, Perdita, although raised as a peasant girl, and Marina, exposed to much worse conditions, always show themselves as truly royal princesses in thought, in speech and in demeanor. Shakespeare never explains why characters as flawed as Leontes and Cymbeline should be entitled to such splendid progeny through simple laws of inheritance. Possibly it is implied (although nowhere stated) that they have started with the same noble inheritance, but that somewhere along the line they have botched it. Possibly Shakespeare simply meant to ascribe the natural royalty of Perdita and the sons of Cymbeline to the permitted magic of this new kind of drama. Possibly he had an allegorical purpose which escapes me.

In any event, he seems to have traveled from naiveté with respect to royal persons to extreme sophistication back to naiveté or something that looks like it. I suspect that he always had a weakness for royalty, making a curious exception for the great Elizabeth on whose death he wrote no elegy (perhaps because she had imprisoned

Southampton). I am sure, anyway, that had he survived to the civil war he would never have been a Roundhead. And I imagine that he would have been proud to have known that the consort of Charles I occupied his house in Stratford for a brief period during those troubled days.

Falstaff and Hal

A FAVORITE DEBATE among Shakespeareans has always been whether or not Prince Hal is unnecessarily harsh with Falstaff at the end of *Henry IV, Part II*. I suppose that to Shakespeare who, for all his ability to place himself in any man's shoes, was a basic conservative, the fat knight may have represented anarchy incarnate. It was all very well to laugh at anarchy, but in the end it had to be put down. Falstaff's world, from the lowest ragamuffin of a pressed soldier to the monarch himself, is made up of potential dupes for Falstaff to cheat. The beauty of his humor is that although absolutely nothing is sacred to him, he knows and mocks the language of veneration of every sect. The laughter that he evokes, if unchecked, might blow away society itself.

Even at his weakest he can be formidable. *The Merry Wives of Windsor* is an inferior play to either part of *Henry IV*, but the first two dialogues between Ford and Falstaff are great comic scenes. Ford starts, like society, with every apparent advantage over his opponent. In the first place he knows who Falstaff is, and Falstaff believes him to be a Mr. Brook. Then he is rich, and Falstaff, as always, is broke, and Ford presumably is a much younger and slenderer man, one possessed (though that may not be saying much) of greater sexual attraction. And finally truth is on Ford's side: his wife *is* loyal; she has no idea of succumbing to her would-be seducer. But Falstaff's magnificent self-assurance reduces all these seeming advantages to nothing. Ford is caught in his own trap. The graphic language in which Falstaff proclaims him a cuckold and then promises him the favors of his own wife shakes Ford's hold on reality and draws him into the terrible world of Falstaff's imagination. And we are almost sucked into it with him. Might not such a stupendous fraud as Falstaff, however ancient, however gross, succeed in seducing Mistress Ford? Indeed, had he addressed her with the force that he addresses her husband, he might have. Surely such a menace to society ought to be punished in the last act. And when he gets presumptuous with royalty, his suppression is a necessity.

But why must he be mixed up with royalty at all? Why cannot his creator associate him exclusively with Fords and Shallows? Why must he be a companion to Prince Hal? Because he was conceived as a companion to Hal. It must be as simple as that. And because to Shakespeare and his contemporaries there was no problem in the simultaneous presentation of comic with serious or even tragic themes.

To my view, admittedly personal, Shakespeare is lacking in taste, or at least adroitness, every time that he places Falstaff and his gang in direct relation to the serious conduct of the civil war. I cannot believe, for example, that Falstaff would ever get a commission; I object to his presence on the battlefield in actual fighting; I am horrified when he hacks the corpse of Hotspur, and I find it ridiculous when Northumberland is told, as a serious item of news, that Sir John has been captured. Worse yet, in *Henry V* I am appalled at the hanging of Bardolph and Nym. On the other hand, left to himself, separated from immediate contrast to the "real," Falstaff is at his most importantly comic when his speech or action provides comment on war: when he talks of honor, when he abuses the King's press, even when he leads his poor ragamuffins where they are "peppered." These latter have no real existence, so their disappearance is not distressing. But Bardolph and Nym are really hanged, just as Hotspur really dies, and their execution jars me as much as if one of the actors on the stage received a real and not a simulated wound.

But this was apparently not so for the Elizabethans. They could laugh their heads off at Falstaff, whether he was fabricating his gorgeous story of the men in buckram or whether he was hoisting the unfortunate Hotspur's corpse on his back, and they could then kick him in the pants as they left the theater, perhaps as a convenient and not unhealthy way of reconverting themselves from fantasy to reality. After all, the old man is an irredeemable liar and lecher; he is a robber in peace and an embezzler in war; he behaves scandalously in battle, and he boasts to all that he will run the kingdom when Hal is crowned. Obviously, if we are going to have to take him seriously, i. e., regard him as a mortal like ourselves, the King's public repudiation of him is mild enough. Be it remembered that Hal has once already saved him from hanging. But I feel no dramatic necessity (speaking, of course, from a different era) in the confrontation of Hal as King with his old friends. Conceding that Falstaff could not possibly be allowed at court, I still do not see why Eastcheap and Windsor have to be brought together. I would never mix up the tavern with the battlefield. But then I delight in Falstaff, and I despise Henry V, at least after he becomes king.

Leaving then the humiliation of Falstaff as a question of taste among generations, agreeable to one that could laugh when a distraught father, hearing of his son's death in battle, cries "Hotspur, Coldspur?" and disagreeable to one that draws a distinction between comic and serious characters and the things that can happen to each, I am still left with the question of whether my dislike of Hal's development into a king is also a question of taste or whether it represents an artistic failure on Shakespeare's part. I suspect that it is a bit of both.

There is no question in my mind, to begin with, that Shakespeare greatly admired Henry V and intended him to appear in all three plays as the very pattern of what a prince and monarch should be. I also believe that shortly afterward Shakespeare came to distrust lovers of war, as witnessed by the deep sense of futility shown in *Troilus and Cressida*, and he may, for all we know, have revised his opinion of warrior kings, but I cannot find the least pacifist sentiment in *Henry V*. I once saw an amateur performance of the play in which the director tried to make use of Bardolph's drunken cry "On, on, on, on, on! to the breach, to the breach!" as a parody of the King's great speech that immediately precedes it, but it was not convincing.

The dramatic scheme of the two parts of *Henry IV* is simple enough: Hal must be brought up from a roisterer to a great king, and Falstaff must be brought down from a comic philosopher to a dirty old man, so that at the end the shedding of Sir John should seem like the blowing away of a last dirty gray cloud to leave a brilliant sun alone in an azure sky. And it almost works out this way. Hal is very splendid, very eloquent in his promises to his dying father and in his assurances to his brothers and to the Lord Chief Justice. But Shakespeare has created such a giant in Falstaff that one begins to sense in *Part II* that he has to push a bit too hard to bring off his plan. Hal has to be turned into a myth and Falstaff into a monster. But not only does Sir John refuse to descend as required by the plot; he keeps Hal from going up. In the end he turns the Prince into a puppet.

The attempt to coarsen Falstaff is evident. Act II ends with Doll Tearsheet sent running to his bedroom in response to Bardolph's shout. Falstaff breaks off a song to tell someone to empty his chamber pot. He exults at the death of Henry IV and boasts that the laws of England will be in his hands, adding a grim: "Woe to My Lord Chief Justice." But so long as Shakespeare allows him any of his original wit, he continues to annihilate the others. When the Prince and Poins disguise themselves as drawers to spy on him, they hear their friendship described in terms that the former cannot altogether laugh away. Doll asks Falstaff why the Prince loves Poins so, and he answers:

> Because their legs are both of a bigness, and a' plays at quoits well, and eats conger and fennel, and drinks off candles' ends for flap-dragons, and rides the wild mare with the boys, and jumps upon joint-stools, and swears with a good grace, and wears his boots very smooth, like unto the sign of the leg, and breeds no bate with telling of discreet stories; and such other gambol faculties a' has, that show a weak mind and an able body, for the which the Prince admits him: for the Prince himself is such another, the weight of a hair will turn the scales between their avoirdupois.

I wonder if I do not pick up a hint of real anger in the Prince's comment to Poins: "Would not this nave of a wheel have his ears cut off?" Such was the penalty for defaming royalty. For there is some truth in Falstaff's description of the Prince's relationship with Poins. Poins is treated very differently from the rest of the gang. He and Hal have a kind of intimacy. In *Part I*, we know from Falstaff that Poins has charm ("If the rascal hath not given me medicines to make me love him, I'll be hanged"); and when the Prince takes his last leave of Boar's Head Tavern to go to the wars, he takes Poins with him, saying:

> By heaven, Poins, I feel me much to blame
> So idly to profane the precious time.

By addressing Poins in verse, he seems to raise him to a rank above the others. It is not, as we shall see, a satisfactory friendship, but it is still a good deal more than Hal has with the others, and I think Falstaff may have caught some of Poins' attraction for him. We do not see Poins again. He does not share in the general humiliation of Act V. Perhaps, like Fenton in *The Merry Wives of Windsor*, he became respectable. But the point is that there is more in common between Hal and Poins than Hal (and possibly Shakespeare) cares to dwell on. Was Hal, assuming the role of a roisterer, altogether assuming a role? Shakespeare's difficulty with the Prince is that if he has any real affection for Falstaff and his companions, he will seem too harsh a judge of them in the end, whereas if he never likes them at all, but uses them purely as a means of his own edification, he will seem too cold and calculating a character. I suspect that Poins' function is to bridge this gap. The Prince is drawn to him, but finds anything like true intimacy impossible.

Let me now trace the attempted development of Hal

into a sovereign which I claim is no more successful than the attempted degradation of Falstaff. In *Part I* Hal is thoroughly attractive throughout. Shakespeare still has plenty of time. The rejection scene is a whole play away. In his first soliloquy Hal assures us of his good intentions for the future, but he does not, as he later does, make the priggish claim that he studies his companions only to know his subjects better, nor does he, as he also later does, falsely accuse Falstaff of being "the tutor and the feeder of my riots." At this point he simply tries to excuse his idle life on the grounds that his subsequent reformation "shall show more goodly and attract more eyes" than it would if it had no foil to set it off. This, incidentally, is an excellent principle for any heir apparent.

Hal is gay in *Part I*, which he never is again, but even in his highest spirits he is no match for Falstaff. His wit is too pedestrian; it falls too quickly into mere abuse. In the scene where they each enact Hal's father, Falstaff carries off the honors by a magnificent apologia for himself that makes Hal's railings seem like the performance of a schoolboy. But at least it is the performance of a pleasant schoolboy. And with his father Hal shows understanding and good manners. He is also decidedly good-natured in procuring Falstaff "a charge of foot" — too much so as it turns out. He is modest and magnanimous over the corpse of Hotspur. When he sees the fallen Falstaff and believes him dead, he seems genuinely affected: "I could have better spared a better man," making us think of Hamlet with Yorick's skull. And when Falstaff comes in alive, bearing on his back the corpse of Hotspur, whom he has the audacity to claim he has killed, Hal is generous enough to say:

> For my part, if a lie may do thee grace,
> I'll gild it with the happiest terms I have.

But in *Part II* Shakespeare has to get on with the job of turning Hal into a king, and the Prince becomes priggish. In Act II, Scene 2, he has a scene with Poins in which he shows a rather Hamletian world-weariness and goes so far as to describe Poins as "one it pleases me, for fault of a better, to call my friend." But Poins lets him down by refusing to believe that his anxiety over his father's illness shows anything but hypocrisy, and Hal must resign himself to the loneliness of his own great nature. There is one more prank at Eastcheap, but the Prince's heart is not in it. He is almost the Hal of *Henry V* now. And when he takes the crown from his father's bedside, I impenitently agree with the old man that he *is* grabby — despite his mistaken belief that death has already entitled him to it. Hal has now become the person who will publicly blame Falstaff for what he has already privately told us was his own scheme. He has become the great monarch who will lead his nation into a purely aggressive war. Shakespeare may have meant us to like him, but I doubt that he has succeeded. For if he had, it would not be necessary to turn the next play into a pageant and Hal into a symbol of national might. He would have had a man to work with.

In the first act of *Henry* V there is no further reference to the crafty advice of Henry IV to his heir that a war abroad might divert attention from the wobbly claim of the House of Lancaster to the throne. Far from it. The hero king must have a better cause than that for his unprovoked invasion of France. And so Shakespeare makes us listen to pages of fustian, torn out of Holinshed, to show that the Salic Law is no proper bar to Henry's claim to the French throne. This genealogical right is strengthened by the Dolphin's taunt of the tennis balls which is supposed to relieve the English King of all responsibility for the bloodbath that follows. So there it is — a theme of unblushing jingoism — and one cannot get away from the fact that Shakespeare either believed it himself or else wrote a piece of deliberate propaganda. I do not care how much fine language there is in *Henry* V. I cannot swallow its subject matter, and I turn from it in dismay.

By so doing I may disqualify myself from having any further valid opinion of the character of Henry V. Indeed, to me he has shrunk to the status of a strutting puppet. But I cannot resist observing that he comes to life just enough to be unpleasant. He is repellent in his threat to the burghers of Harfleur that his army will rape their daughters. He is heartless in approving the hanging of his old friend Bardolph. He is sententious about the grave responsibility that he carries for a war entirely initiated by himself and falsely modest when he tells the French princess that he is a rough soldier who can woo her only in blunt terms. But perhaps London audiences in 1599 found him entrancing. At any rate, he was created for them and not for me.

The play is a sorry tribute to the might of Falstaff. It comes to life only for a minute in the tale of his death. We have seen what has happened to his old friend Hal without him; Bardolph, Nym and Pistol are sordid echoes of their old comic selves. Fluellen is introduced to bolster the sagging comedy scenes, but Fluellen to me is less funny even than Doctor Caius in *The Merry Wives of Windsor*. The characters are like the gods in Valhalla after the abduction of Freya. They have lost their youth and freshness.

The Last Comedies

When Shakespeare's company hired Blackfriars' Theatre, in addition to the Globe, so that they could perform in winter as well as summer, they needed a different kind of drama for a more aristocratic audience. The comedy coming into fashionable vogue was of a fanciful, romantic nature, filled with mystery, with magic, with quixotic behavior, the type that Beaumont and Fletcher were to make so popular. Evidently the better sort wanted to be amused without being too concerned, and excited without being too depressed. They were perfectly willing to have the characters done to death, but they liked them to come alive again in the end.

Now one of the reasons that Shakespeare showed so much more variety than any other playwright was that he so thoroughly knew his business of pleasing. He was always perfectly willing to turn his hand to a new taste, and he could usually do what he wanted with it. I would even go so far as to speculate that he saw in the romantic comedy a method of expressing truths about human nature quite as profound as that of tragedy. He could use the sudden darkness of inexplicable human perversity to cover the bright sky of the comic world with an effect as striking as the rage of Lear on the heath.

Much earlier he had experimented with such contrasts. *Romeo and Juliet* is sometimes seen as a drama, whose tragedy is brought on by the lovers' impetuousness, but to my mind the term "star-crossed" is more explanatory. The lovers sense their doom, but not through any fault of their own. Romeo has a foreboding of "untimely death" on the threshold of the Capulets' palace; he fears "some consequence yet hanging in the stars." Juliet, looking down on him from her balcony, imagines that she sees him in his tomb. But the lovers give themselves over to their love, anyway, and I do not see that Shakespeare ever implies that they are wrong to do so. I think he wholly approves when Romeo says:

> But come what sorrow can,
> It cannot countervail the exchange of joy
> That one short minute gives me in her sight.
> Do thou but close our hands with holy words,
> Then love-devouring death do what he dare,
> It is enough I may but call her mine.

When Friar Laurence replies that violent delights have violent ends, he is only stating a truism. He proceeds with the marriage, counselling them to "love moderately." But the lovers will never have the chance to learn this. They will never have more than one night. And even at that, perhaps they have more than anyone else in hot, quarrelsome Verona. Would they have been any better off had they postponed the marriage? Would they ever have got around the Paris marriage? Was it Romeo's fault that Tybalt forced him into a duel? Was it Juliet's that Friar Laurence's message never got through? No. The cards are against them from the beginning, and they are lucky, under the circumstances, to have had as much as they have.

And what are these circumstances? The lovers are pitted against madmen. Juliet's hateful old father, with the help of the duel-loving Tybalt, causes all the trouble in the play. Capulet is an arbitrary, pigheaded ass, the type that causes half the trouble in the world. He does not even act for his own advantage. He will marry Juliet to Paris largely because she objects.

So Shakespeare's suspicion, even as a young writer, that many of our mortal ills are caused by "motiveless malignity" became confirmed with middle age. Does Macbeth really want to be King of Scotland? Does Lear really want to banish Cordelia? Does Coriolanus want to cause civil war? Do the Trojans care about keeping Helen? Or is there in all of these tragedies a deeper motivation, the human impulse toward self-destruction?

Pericles, Shakespeare's first effort in the new manner, need not occupy us here. As a play it is a failure, rambling and diffuse, valuable to its author only as a blueprint for *The Winter's Tale*. *Cymbeline*, the second attempt, is one of Shakespeare's great achievements — up to the awakening of Imogen by Cloten's headless corpse. After that it goes to pieces, and goes to pieces in just the parts that most call for the new Fletcherian treatment: the final battle, the prison scene with Posthumus' vision and the denouement with England's unexpected decision to pay the Roman tribute. Unsympathetic as I am with G. B. Shaw's general attitude toward Shakespeare, I can understand his composing his own Act V.

What happened? Did Shakespeare get tired or sick? After writing the incomparable scenes of Posthumus' wager, of Imogen and Iachimo, of the King's sons in the wilderness, scenes that made the play a favorite with such different poets as Keats and Tennyson (the latter's copy was buried with him), did he turn the rest over to juniors? The plotting is confused, the minor characters inconsistently drawn. Why should the Queen and Cloten be suddenly shown as patriots? Could the Shakespeare who mapped out *Macbeth* really think of no better way to put Imogen into a deathlike sleep than to have her suddenly take sick and swallow the contents of a box that Pisanio and she believe to be a medicine but which is actually a sleeping potion substituted by Cornelius for the poison that the Queen, planning to murder Pisanio, has intended to put in it? And how is an audience meant to react to Imogen's taking the dead Cloten's "foot Mercurial" and "Martial thigh" for her own husband's? Is it possible that a laugh was intended here? I am very much afraid that it was.

Yet for all of this, I think, with the exception of Posthumus' vision, that even the last act has a Shakespearean ring. Perhaps Shakespeare was simply not yet at ease with his new form. The contrast of evil with good, at any rate, was there. *Pericles* and *Cymbeline* have the striking antithesis of black perversity with radiant innocence, of Antiochus' incest with Pericles' romantic love, of the bawdry of the pimps with the purity of Marina, of Iachimo's fiendishness with Imogen's fineness and courage. But Shakespeare had not yet found the vehicle for its perfect expression. This he was to find in his last two plays.

In the bright atmosphere of the first act of *The Winter's* Tale everything points to happiness. King Leontes has a beautiful and loving wife, a devoted friend willing to leave his own kingdom for a nine months' visit, a charming son and heir, a peaceful kingdom — everything a man or monarch could want. But what of that? The finer it all is, the stronger the impulse to destroy it. Shakespeare finds here the perfect tool in romantic comedy to express the contrast between the idyllic atmosphere of the court and the black horror of Leontes' passion.

For Leontes needs no Iago to stir him on, no evidence to inflame his jealousy. His fit is totally perverse. He is unable, despite the number of sycophants who habitually attach themselves to Shakespearean princes, to find a single courtier who is willing even to pretend to take his side. The enormity of his accusation appalls even the worst toadies.

But Leontes clings to it. He *wants* to believe Hermione guilty, even though, on one level of his consciousness, he must know that she is innocent. He threatens all who take her side with dire punishment, and when the oracle that he himself has invoked speaks against him, he denies the validity of its utterance. Only when his son dies does the reality of what he is doing at last break in upon him, and then he turns to the cloudy satisfaction of sackcloth and ashes and greedily heaps guilt after guilt upon his guilty head.

The sixteen-year break returns us to light and air. Florizel and Perdita show us how easily humans may be happy. Never once does Florizel waver in his fidelity; he is perfectly willing to give up his future crown for his love. In this he is justified by his royal divination of Perdita's high birth. Presumably he would not be so sympathetic to an aristocratic Jacobean audience if he were willing to renounce his royal responsibilities for a *real* peasant. Modern critics, misliking magic, can try to read something else into this, but I am perfectly willing to accept this stage convention in the later plays and recognize that the goodness of Florizel and Perdita is in part an inherited fineness innate in royal bloodstreams (cf. Arviragus and Guiderius in *Cymbeline*).

The irrational strikes again with Polixenes who demontrates a shocking temper at the discovery of Florizel's plans to marry a peasant girl. Now Shakespeare has a bit of a problem here, for Polixenes has surely some justification in opposing so inappropriate a match secretly undertaken by his only son. He has to be brought closer to the case of Leontes by his rudeness to Perdita and by his savage threats to the old shepherd. And perhaps, too, he shows the flaw in his character by failing to respond to the royalty of Perdita as his more finely intuitive son does. If he were not so perverse, he would know that she was a king's child.

Camillo comes to the rescue, his task made easier by the fact that Florizel and Perdita never falter in their resolution. Why should they? They are good and they are right, and they know it. In the splendid last scene human wickedness has been expiated, and we have a glimpse of happiness to come. It is all quite delightful and impossible. Where could it happen but in a fairyland? And yet is it so difficult to achieve? Is it so difficult *not* to be Leontes?

In *The Tempest* Shakespeare supplies the conventional motivation of ambition for the wicked characters of the play. Antonio has usurped the throne of Milan out of ambition, and he has been assisted in his wicked project by Alonso, King of Naples, in return for the submission of Milan to the domination of Naples. Sebastian, brother to Alonso, enters into a conspiracy with Antonio to kill the King, again for obvious motives of ambition. Yet the fact that the scheming for the murder of the King occurs in the unreal atmosphere of the island gives to the activities of the conspirators much of that atmosphere of willful perversity that we find in *The Winter's Tale.* How small, how petty, how vicious, how almost pathetic Antonio and Sebastian seem in their plots to achieve the rule of a distant kingdom to which, marooned, they have not even the power to return! Shakespeare, at the end of his career, had found the most effective way of dramatizing the early simple thought of Puck in *A Midsummer Night's Dream:* "Lord, what fools these mortals be!" He had only to cast a group of such mortals ashore on an enchanted island where another mortal has brought order out of nature by moral and magic power.

In this way the comic wicked characters are seen in very much the same light as the serious wicked characters. Stephano and Trinculo in their drunken plot to kill Prospero are only slightly more ridiculous than Antonio and Sebastian. Prospero towers so high in moral stature above all four that there is little to choose between them. And, once again, these foolish, wicked, blinded plotters are placed in contrast to what man *could* be: to Miranda and Ferdinand, who, like Perdita and Florizel, shine in physical and moral beauty. Again the note is struck that men have to go out of their way to make life odious. But they always will. And one does not feel that Prospero has any very real optimism that matters are going to be so different when they all get back again to Milan or Naples. He must always remember his failure with Caliban.

For Caliban, Shakespeare's only monster, ends a long series of studies in evil. Yet with Caliban there is a difference. He is not a sadist. Unlike Aaron or Iago or Don John he takes no satisfaction in villainy. He is simply man reduced to the level of animal. His crime in Prospero's eyes is to attempt to violate the honor of Miranda, but to Caliban there is no such thing as honor. He responds to the girl as any dog would to any bitch. Chastised for this, he predictably takes advantage of all opportunities to destroy Prospero and recover his island. His existence is intensely irritating to Prospero because he symbolizes the brute part of man that no amount of philosophy, or discipline, or religion, or even magic can ever eradicate. Every victory of Prospero's must be tempered by the knowledge that Caliban has to be kept under constant restraint. Once he lets him go and turns his back, he can expect that nail of which Caliban speaks to Stephano to be hammered into his skull.

But Prospero does not turn his back, or at least does so only for a moment. He is art and wisdom: Caliban is flesh, and the balance is maintained, always consciously. There is even a kind of partnership between the two: Prospero admits to needing Caliban's help about the house, and Caliban in the end concedes: "How fine my master is!" Prospero may be unlovable, but so is Caliban unhatable. After all, it *was* his island, and one admires his superiority to Stephano and Trinculo when they are distracted from their lethal purpose by what he properly calls the trash of the trumpery costumes.

To love and hate one must go beyond magic and the enchanted island. Neither Prospero nor Caliban is quite human, but Miranda and Ferdinand, both lovable, are, and Antonio and Sebastian, equally unlovable, also are. But Miranda and Ferdinand are idealized humans; they would be just a bit too good to be true, like Perdita and Florizel, outside their enchanted domain. Not so the other two. They are only too credible. Shakespeare in the end had the same terrible view of Coleridge's "malignity" that he had in the beginning. Only he had placed it like a death's head on a valentine.

The Sonnets— A Thousandth Theory

A CHARACTERISTIC that I have noted of many essays and books about Shakespeare's sonnets is that they start by scolding the reader for any irrelevant curiosity as to the identities of the "Mr. W. H." of Thomas Thorpe's famous dedication, or of the fair youth, the rival poet and the dark mistress. What does it matter? these commentators ask us. Do we not have the sonnets themselves? What does it signify whether they were written as literary exercises, as a fictional sequence or as the deepest expression of the poet's heart? Are they not here before us, works of art, for us to enjoy?

But having said all this, some of these same commentators proceed themselves to dabble in theories. Who can blame them? It is irresistible. Here are 154 sonnets of the greatest English poet, possibly the greatest literary figure in history, and they constitute the only hint or fragment of an autobiography that we have. Not a letter, not a note, hardly a recorded conversation survives, nothing but a series of legal documents showing the poet's increasing financial prosperity, a body of dramatic work that is highly impersonal, a record of theatrical appearances and a will. I think that the man who does not try to probe the sonnets for traces of the poet's heart or personality is a critic austere to the point of inhumanity.

My friend A. L. Rowse has recently subjected the Southampton theory to a very precise dating. He argues that all 154 sonnets published by Thorpe in 1609 were written in the chronological order in which they appear and in honor of Shakespeare's first patron, and that they were composed between the years 1592 and 1595. He maintains that they start with the 17 sonnets urging the young Earl to marry—his mother, apparently, was anxious to have him carry out his betrothal to a granddaughter of Lord Burleigh. Sonnets 18 through 39 are conventional, flattering poems proclaiming the young Earl's immortality through Shakespeare's verse. But Sonnets 40 through 42 take on a much more personal note. The young peer has apparently been seduced by Shakespeare's mistress. Throughout the whole sonnet sequence it is clear that the author's feeling for this mistress, the famous "Dark Woman" of the later poems, is a purely physical passion, while his adoration of the young man is meant to be interpreted on a higher spiritual plane. Sonnets 43 through 75 are again conventional duty sonnets, with some advice against the Earl's keeping of bad company. Sonnets 76 through 86 deal with a rival poet whom Rowse identifies as Christopher Marlowe. Because Sonnet 86 is couched in the past tense, Rowse suggests that it refers to Marlowe's death in 1593. Sonnets 87 through 126 speak of the sad possibility that the poet's profession as an actor may be an embarrassment to his patron, and 117 through 122 seem to indicate that the poet himself has been in some way unfaithful to Southampton. The remaining sonnets, 126 through 154, are addressed to the poet's mistress, but because of the insulting language in which he complains of his physical bondage and of her own sexual looseness, it is Rowse's theory that they were written for the delectation of Southampton and his circle of young gallants rather than for the lady herself.

It is all extremely interesting and not illogical, but we must remember that it is entirely hypothetical. We do not, for example, even know that Shakespeare ever met the Earl of Southampton. It seems probable that he did, because of the warmth in the language of the dedication of *The Rape of Lucrece*, but it is still possible that permission for the dedication could have been granted to a grateful and enthusiastic young poet without an audience.

My insuperable stumbling block, however, with Rowse comes over the famous "dating" sonnet, 107, and the four lines which have probably occasioned more comment than any other four lines in Shakespeare:

> The mortal moon hath her eclipse endured,
> And the sad augurs mock their own presage;
> Incertainties now crown themselves assured,
> And peace proclaims olives of endless age.

Pretty well every serious critic has agreed that the mortal moon is Queen Elizabeth herself, and Rowse maintains that her eclipse was the conspiracy by her physician, Dr. Lopez, and others, to assassinate her and that the peace was the victory in France of Henry of Navarre and consequent end of the religious wars. But try as I may, I cannot see why a conspiracy should "eclipse" a monarch. While nobody knew of it, the Queen could hardly be said to be in darkness, and with its discovery and prevention, the darkness was avoided. Where then was the eclipse? As to the victory of Henry of Navarre, one has only to read *The Elizabethan Journals* by G. B. Harrison to see that this was not followed by any immediate cessation of hostilities. The fighting in France continued for years.

Shakespeare used the word "endured" in the sense of "suffered" in *King Lear*, and in *Antony and Cleopatra* Antony's reference to the eclipse of the "terrene moon" (Cleopatra) refers not to her temporary disappearance behind another celestial body, but to her end.

Therefore, I join the commentators who believe that this quatrain must refer to the death of Queen Elizabeth in 1603. The accession of James I was followed by peace with Spain and a general explosion of jubilation and hope. People had very much feared the possibility of civil war on the old Queen's death, and even those who had most confidently predicted disaster must have been overjoyed to have been proved wrong. Hence, the sad augurs "mocked" their own presage.

Mr. J. B. Leishman has pointed out a remarkable parallel in a sonnet by Drayton published in 1605, where precisely the same thought is more specifically stated:

> Lastly mine eyes amazedly have seen
> Essex's great fall, Tyrone his peace to gain,
> The quiet end of that long-living Queen
> The King's fair entrance and our peace with Spain.

I can now start my own theorizing (for in this field nobody, let alone the angels, fears to tread) by listing what to me are the facts and what to me are the likelihoods. Here are the facts:

(1) Sonnet 138: "When my love swears that she is made of truth" and Sonnet 144: "Two loves I have, of comfort and despair" were published in 1599 in *A Passionate Pilgrim.*

(2) The balance of the known sonnets of Shakespeare (excluding those in the plays) were published in 1609 with a dedication to a "Mr. W. H.," the meaning of which has never been deciphered.

(3) Some of the 1609 sonnets are addressed to a handsome young man or men; others to a dark-complexioned woman of loose morals.

(4) The relationship with one young man lasted at least three years (Sonnet 104).

Here are what I consider the likelihoods:

(1) The writing of the sonnets, judging from variations of style, covers a period of possibly a dozen years, from 1592 to 1604.

(2) The first 17 sonnets belong in a group and could

only have been written to a young peer of great family, as there is no conceivable reason that he should be so strongly urged to beget a son unless he had an important title to pass on. These sonnets are early in style and may well have been written to Southampton in 1592.

(3) For all that has been said of the Elizabethan custom of gentlemen addressing themselves in what to us are romantic terms, it is still difficult for me to conceive that Shakespeare, a mere actor, would describe a great peer as "the master-mistress" of his passion, or that he would refer openly to Southampton's sexual organs, as he does in Sonnet 20. Nor can I believe that Shakespeare would have used the phrase "thou doest common grow" to an earl, as he does in Sonnet 69.

(4) The rival poet sonnets, like the first 17, must have been also addressed to a peer. Who but a great nobleman and patron would have had poems dedicated to him? This peer could have also been Southampton, but he might have been the Earl of Pembroke. The style seems to me to be more mature than that of the "marriage" sonnets. Also, I see no reason why the poet should not as easily have been George Chapman as Marlowe. We all remember how impressed Keats was by the great sweep of Chapman's poetry. Compare *On First Looking into Chapman's Homer* with Sonnet 86: "Was it the proud full sail of his great verse."

(5) The sonnets to the dark mistress, 126 *et seq.*, although late in Thorpe's chronology, have so many simi-

larities to *Love's Labour's Lost* that I would date them early in the series, and I suspect that those which deal with her seduction of the young man, 133 through 140, refer to the same incident covered in Sonnets 40 through 42. But it does not have to follow that the young man was Southampton or Pembroke or Shakespeare's patron or even a nobleman. Furthermore, because of the punning in Sonnet 135, I feel sure that the young man's name, like Shakespeare's, was Will. This was not Southampton's Christian name, though it was Pembroke's (William Herbert), but I doubt that anyone called Pembroke by it.

(6) Sonnets 117 through 122, which show the poet's guilt over some kind of infidelity to a young man, seem couched in very different spirit from the more subservient earlier sonnets to the young man whom Shakespeare's mistress seduced. There is no idea in these earlier sonnets of any fault on Shakespeare's part. Nor can I imagine that Shakespeare would admit any infidelity to a noble patron in a duty sonnet.

(7) Sonnet 145, in octosyllabic lines, seems to me utterly out of place in the whole series and possibly not by Shakespeare at all.

(8) Sonnet 146, dealing with the poet's soul, seems to me to be Shakespeare's, but not to belong in the series. It is very interesting as the only instance in his poetry that gives any hint of personal religiosity.

(9) Sonnets 153 and 154 deal with the healing waters

of Bath and seem to be quite extraneous to the entire collection.

✧

What then do I make of this tissue of fact and possibility? I suggest that the 1609 collection is a series of sonnets written to several different people over a period of ten to a dozen years. I do not believe that a romantic affection for one young man would have lasted so long a period.

I have already touched on the question of homosexuality in the sonnets in my essay on *Troilus and Cressida*. The term is unfortunate because it tends, even in our liberal era, to introduce so many prejudices and defenses. Some day, no doubt, the different degrees of love, physical and otherwise, between members of the same sex and of the opposite will be classified without irrelevant emotional reactions. I suspect that Shakespeare's sexual directions were divided more or less evenly between the sexes: that he enjoyed physical intercourse with women, perhaps rather coarse ones, but that he did not find in it the spiritual elevation that he sought, usually with disillusionment, in the cultivation of handsome youths. Fidelity, so elusive, became a fetish with him. Julia, Rosalind, Portia, Viola, Imogen were all played by boys and masqueraded as boys, and all are defined in terms of their perfect fidelity to their lovers. Whether, as Shakespeare grew older, these relationships with young men remained entirely platonic may be doubted, for I find his references to his own "wretched errors" and "madding fever" in Sonnets 117 through 121 enigmatic, to say the least, but there is nothing definite to go on in this respect, and it seems likely that at the time he wrote *Troilus* (1601–1602) he regarded any physical connection between men with extreme distaste.

But what to me is important in all of this is the duration of such friendships. Physical beauty is of even greater importance in romantic male friendships than it is in heterosexual relations: a young man's loss of hair or gaining of weight may be fatal to his admirer's illusion, and the older man is in constant apprehension of falling into decrepitude. It is observed in the *New Variorum Edition* that the word "time" occurs on seventy-eight occasions in Sonnets 1—126 (those addressed to the young man or men) and not once in the balance to the dark mistress. This sense of panic at passing time and this clutching at the consoling permanence of art has been beautifully caught by Tennessee Williams in the relationship which he describes in *Sweet Bird of Youth* between an aging actress and a tough young man (a relationship, like so many in Williams' plays, that seems to have been converted from a homosexual to a heterosexual one for stage purposes) and in the scene where the actress triumphantly affirms the superiority of her art to her lover's mere youth. There is a good bit of this in the sonnets.

I also find it significant that Francis Meres in *Palladis Tamia* (1598) speaks of Shakespeare's "sugared sonnets among his private friends." Now, of course, we do not know that these sonnets, or any of them, were included in the 1609 edition, but there is certainly no reason that they should not have been, and if they were, it is at least some evidence that the 1609 series does not tell a single story of a single friendship.

My simple deduction from the period of time over which I believe the sonnets to have been written is that they were addressed to at least five persons: two patrons, two young men and the dark mistress. I should suggest the following assignments:

(1) Sonnets 1 through 17 are very early, perhaps as early as 1592, and are dedicated to a young peer urging him to marry. Sonnet 26, "Lord of my love," is possibly an *envoi* to this series.

(2) Sonnets 18 through 25, 27 through 74, and 127 through 152 (excluding 145 and 146) all strike me as dealing with an episode in the early or middle 1590's and involve a woman of dark complexion and a young man of some social position superior to Shakespeare's but not anything like the rank of earl. That this young man's name was Will and that he was seduced by the dark woman who was also Shakespeare's mistress, causing some distress amid the trio, seems evident, but the woman was obviously so loose that Shakespeare reconciled himself to sharing her not only with his friend but with many others. There is pain and sadness in this triple relationship but nothing like the agony that is to come in the

later sonnets. I agree with Oscar Wilde in his *The Portrait of Mr. W. H.* where he points out that Sonnet 25 could not have been written to a great peer as the young man is excluded from the category of "great princes." Now even though Southampton was not a prince, in the language of hyperbole of sonnets, it would not have been polite to say so.

(3) Sonnets 75 through 86 are to a patron, probably, from their style, a later one than Southampton, perhaps Pembroke.

(4) Sonnets 87 through 126, which to me contain the greatest of the collection, may deal with a second young man, of high but not necessarily exalted birth, whom I seem to make out as one of those charming, cool-hearted, seemingly warm persons who inspire great love without (quite involuntarily) being able to return it in the same degree. Shakespeare was in his late thirties when he met him, perhaps as late as 1600, and I conceive the friendship to have been more passionate than the earlier one and filled with more intense suffering. There seems to have been infidelity, or at least unkindness, on both sides, and Shakespeare speaks of having been off with "unknown minds" and having "hoisted sail to all the winds." He may have been driven in sheer frustration to seek other and dubious alliances:

> Alas! 'tis true I have gone here and there
> And made myself a motley to the view,
> Gored mine own thoughts, sold cheap what is most dear,

Made old offences of affections new.
Most true it is that I have looked on truth
Askance and strangely:

And again:

Even so, being full of your ne'er-cloying sweetness,
To bitter sauces did I frame my feeding;
And, sick of welfare, found a kind of meetness
To be diseased ere that there was true needing.

I doubt if these "affections new" were with women, because in the kind of intense relationship that existed between the two men (and whether or not it was what we would call a homosexual one), an affair with a woman would not have constituted such a disloyalty as the cultivation of another young man.

The near hysteria of Sonnet 90 seems close in mood to *Hamlet.* One can imagine, with J. B. Leishman, the Prince spitting out these quatrains to Horatio, had he had reason to suspect that the latter, like Rosencrantz and Guildenstern, was in the pay of the King:

Then hate me when thou wilt — if ever, now —
Now, while the world is bent my deeds to cross,
Join with the spite of Fortune, make me bow,
And do not drop in for an afterloss.
Ah, do not, when my heart hath scaped this sorrow,
Come in the rearward of a conquered woe;
Give not a windy night a rainy morrow,
To linger out a purposed overthrow.

I cannot believe that these lines could have been written as early in the poet's career as Rowse places them.

Sonnet 116 is probably the most splendid of the whole series with its mighty invocation to love:

> Let me not to the marriage of true minds
> Admit impediments; love is not love
> Which alters when it alteration finds,
> Or bends with the remover to remove,
> Oh, no, it is an ever-fixed mark,
> That looks on tempests and is never shaken;
> It is the star to every wand'ring bark,
> Whose worth's unknown, although his height be taken.

It is noticeable in this sonnet as in Sonnet 94, to which it may be a kind of antiphone, that there is no reference to any loved one, man or woman:

> They that have pow'r to hurt and will do none,
> That do not do the thing they most do show,
> Who, moving others, are themselves as stone,
> Unmoved, cold, and to temptation slow:
> They rightly do inherit heaven's graces,
> And husband Nature's riches from expense;
> They are the lords and owners of their faces,
> Others but stewards of their excellence.

Yet to me they are the most deeply felt poems of the whole series. There is a respect, an admiration and a melancholy love in the ironic praise of the young man who is the lord and owner of his face, but there is pity, too. Shakespeare may be glad enough to be the steward of his friend's excellence, but he knows that in knowing love, or even in glimpsing it, he has something that is worth more than the saving of all of Nature's riches.

◆

How did Thorpe get the sonnets? We shall never know, I am sure, but I disagree with the many commentators who feel that Shakespeare could not have had a hand in it. Certainly, he did not edit or correct the text; there are too many errors and confusing juxtapositions of sonnets. But I cannot conceive who could have gathered them all together without the poet's help. Perhaps he wanted them published. We know what care he took with *Venus and Adonis* and *The Rape of Lucrece*. Immortality in those days was believed more assured by poetry than by drama. And what would he have had to fear from autobiographical implications? They are so veiled that three centuries of scholarship have not unraveled them. Why should he not have assumed that his readers would take them as fiction — as indeed his biographer Sir Sidney Lee did?

Perhaps the second young man was Mr. W. H. Perhaps he persuaded Shakespeare to let him have all the sonnets, those to himself and to others, to weave into a series. What poet, after all, would not have been pleased to see them in print?

Racine and Shakespeare—Another Look

RACINE AND SHAKESPEARE, since the dawn of romanticism in France, have been regarded as opposites, and certainly, from the point of view of a neoclassicist, they are. It is difficult for us today even to comprehend that critics once took the tragic unities very seriously indeed, but to those who cared about them, Shakespeare was obviously a barbarian. To a modern eye that pushes aside nice questions of time, place and even of action, *Phèdre* and *Macbeth*, once two different poles, meet on a common equator of passion.

Yet if we have straightened out the perspective from a theatrical point of view, we may have clouded it from a moral one. We live today, even if we are atheists at heart, in a world that holds salvation to be obtainable not by faith or works but by deeds alone. Lord Melbourne said that he liked the Order of the Garter because it had no nonsense about merit. No remark could have set him further apart from us, to whom merit is everything. The sons of famous men change their names to be "on their own," and the heirs of fortunes try to look as if they had earned them by the sweat of their brows. One even hears it said as a truism that the man who overcomes fear is braver than the man who feels none.

On the other end of the moral scale, we hold that shame, too, must be earned, that no act is a sin unless consciously committed. It was my difficulty with tragedy that, as a child of the "fault" era, I persisted in seeking a "tragic flaw" in the protagonist to give a clue to the ultimate catastrophe. I saw the crime of Phèdre, not in her illicit passion for her stepson, but in the action in which her surrender to this passion involves her. Phèdre to me became a monster like Macbeth, transformed by love into a murderess, as the Scottish thane was transformed by ambition into a bloody tyrant. I could not accept the idea that a person could be wicked simply for *feeling* an incestuous desire. So long as the emotion was bottled up, how could there be evil?

But I have come to believe that Shakespeare and Racine believed in wickedness quite apart from the act of wickedness. Theologically, the intent is as much a crime as the execution. It is only in a Freudian era that we believe that we are not responsible for our thoughts and impulses. Macbeth is wicked before he comes on stage. The witches know that. And when I saw Marie Bell's *Phèdre*, I understood at last that Phèdre's crime is not what she does but what she *is*.

> Le ciel mit dans mon sein une flamme funeste,
> La détestable Oenone a conduit tout le reste.

That is Phèdre's dying explanation of what has happened, and I believe that it is meant to be taken as the true one. The age of Louis XIV was an age of absolutes. It did not want its heroes (Horace, the Cid) to struggle to be heroes, and it certainly did not want its heroines to have to struggle to be chaste.

Step by step, Racine demonstrates how little responsibility Phèdre bears for the death of Hippolyte. Like her mother before her, she is a victim of Venus' spite. She struggles valiantly against her passion, to the extent of banishing Hippolyte from Athens to Trézène. Ironically Trézène turns out to be the very abode in which her husband, Thésée, places her, before he sets off on one of his shady enterprises. At the end of her rope now, wasted by passion and yearning for death, Phèdre at last confesses her love to Oenone, her inquisitive old busybody of a companion. No sooner has she done so than a messenger comes in with the tidings (false, as it turns out) of Thésée's death.

Oenone then persuades her, as a helpless widow, to appeal to her stepson for political protection, and in the ensuing scene Phèdre, of course, blurts out her true feelings and horrifies the young man. Next she hears that Thésée is not only alive but about to appear on the scene. Terrified that Hippolyte will denounce her, she allows Oenone (whose wicked idea it is) to denounce him first. Oenone assures her that Thésée in punishing his son will show a father's leniency. When this turns out not to be so, Phèdre hurries to Thésée, meaning to confess all, if necessary, to save Hippolyte, but before she can do so, she receives the news that the supposedly misogynist youth has all along been in love with Aricie. Before she can recover her wits from this blow, Hippolyte is dead. Phèdre then does all that any woman could do. She clears his name and poisons herself.

To Racine, the crimes of the play are less in the action than in the soul. Slander and murder are the lesser evils which may be expected to flow from the moral gangrene of an incestuous love. And all his characters see it the same way. Even the cynical, worldly-wise Oenone cries "Oh, crime!" when she first hears of Phèdre's passion. Hippolyte considers Phèdre as bad as her mother, who ran after a bull. Thésée does not even shudder when Phèdre dies; another monster has been eliminated, that is all. It is difficult for us to get quite so aroused over an incest where no consanguinity is involved, but this difficulty is nothing compared to our difficulty in accepting as a sin what seems to us to be simply a temptation to sin.

Yet Phèdre herself accepts this opinion. She is as revolted by the passion within herself as are the other characters. She may hurl epithets at the implacable goddess who has undone her family, but the fact that she is the plaything of a cruel divinity does not in any way diminish in her eyes her own moral turpitude. An ugly character is like an ugly face, no less offensive for being wished upon the wearer. Phèdre is a soul from whom divine grace has been withdrawn. Like an unbaptized child or a human being born before Christ, she is denied forever the joys of the elect.

What then, except for the exquisite verse, is there in this tragedy for the modern reader who does not believe in a God who withdraws his grace arbitrarily, or in the inherent wickedness of any passion so long as it is restrained? There is, quite simply, the vivid sense of guilt — that guilt that is still universal. No matter what our reason tells us, most of us have felt, at one time or another, especially in our younger years, a loathing and shame for something within ourselves for which we are not responsible, but which still makes us feel monsters. Who has not speculated, like Phèdre, that the only reason he is greeted with smiles and not horror, is that his fellow men do not know of the evil within him? Who has not felt that his mask was a better thing than himself?

Another criticism of the play is that the young lovers are stilted, that Hippolyte and Aricie are a cardboard pair acting out a conventional romance in a formal French garden. But isn't that just the way the normal world appears to the guilt-ridden? The proper lovers bow, pirouette and coo; old Thésée boasts of his shoddy exploits; Théramène, Hippolyte's tutor, orates windily about past heroics. They may seem like puppets, but how blissful a state of puppetry must appear to a soul on fire.

> Tous les jours se levent clairs et sereins pour eux!

This cry from the heart of Phèdre as she thinks of the peace of mind which the young lovers, even cruelly separated, enjoy, is reminiscent of the agony of Macbeth as he watches the slow, dignified procession of Banquo's descendants bearing their regalia of royalty. It is the Day of Wrath.